"Grand stories on learning and innovation at the crossroads of serendipity."

Katy Borner, PhD,
Victor H. Yngve Professor of Engineering & Information Science,
Indiana University at Bloomington, USA

"If you seek to learn from a master, then Bill Rouse is your dream teacher. He is a renaissance person who combines deep technical skills in mathematical modeling analysis of complex human-run systems with comparable knowledge of broad system context — with all its complexities and nuances. His book marches through his life experiences, providing lessons learned — with his many successes and a few misses. His life adventures demonstrate vividly how one should embrace taking risks, delving deeply into new and complex new problem areas, even when having no previous experience on those problems. The structured analytical approach leads to innovative solutions."

Richard C. Larson, PhD,
Mitsui Professor of Data, Systems, and Society, MIT, USA

"Wise and technically sophisticated, practical and insightful, and based on an overwhelming amount of personal research and practical implementation, Bill Rouse has provided us with a 50-year perspective on problem solving using both advanced mathematical modeling and careful attention to human needs, aspirations, and requirements. For those interested in dysfunction, crises, and subsequent change for the better, Rouse's models, analysis, and extensive examples offer a primer for process, analysis, and action, emphasizing always the imperative to understand the who, what, how, and why of every challenge or opportunity. His deep personal and successful engagement in multiple initiatives, enterprises, and consultancies has given Rouse a unique perspective, and his multiple publications testify to the impact of these experiences. Numerous real-world cases provide the opportunity for this development of a complex, if fundamental, set of guidelines for addressing the challenges of private, public, and systemic enterprises. This book is required reading for those who want to understand the system imperatives for enhanced performance both now and in the future."

John V. Lombardi, PhD,
President Emeritus, University of Florida, USA

"In this empowering and enlightening book, Bill Rouse takes us on a journey into his exemplary engineering mind and works, providing views into complex systems and a vision for managing them effectively."

Guru Madhavan, PhD
Norman R. Augustine Senior Scholar and Senior Director of Programs,
National Academy of Engineering,
Author of Applied Minds: How Engineers Think

"A technical page-turner, probably the only engineering book that you will read cover to cover. With this professional memoir, Bill Rouse weaves intriguing personal and professional history – as vital context – into 'how and why' so many of his multitudes of projects progressed so successfully from concept to full strategic adoption. The 'play-by-play' project descriptions, illuminated with fascinating 'color commentary,' provide hard-earned project management insight in a literary fashion that even non-scientists will breeze through, feeling one 'I'll be darn' after another."

Dennis K. McBride, PhD,
President Emeritus, Potomac Institute for Policy Studies, USA

"Few people are as well-equipped as Bill Rouse to write such a remarkable compendium, not only of innovations today, but of how we got there and where we might be going in the future. His vast personal experience in multiple areas and his mastery of systems analysis allowed him to provide a global vision of evolution of technologies and societies and to link such diverse domains as technologies, business, medicine, and human behaviors. This vast perspective allows him to capture the enormous transformations of societies and the future possibilities. Indeed, this is a unique book that should enrich social perspectives, and support key decisions about policies made today, that will affect our future and that of our children."

Elisabeth Pate-Cornell, PhD,
Burt and Deedee McMurtry Professor,
Department of Management Science and Engineering,
Stanford University, USA

"An insightful presentation on how to derive impactful contributions to society, organizations and individuals based on the distinguished scholarly and practical experience of the author."

Gavriel Salvendy, PhD,
University Distinguished Professor,
University of Central Florida, Founding President,
Academy of Science, Engineering and Medicine of Florida, USA

"Bill Rouse is a system modeler par excellence. He has provided us with a review of his professional career combined with a description of his modeling achievements in multiple domains, ranging from human-interaction with low level systems, business and government enterprises, and large-scale societal systems such as health care. In each case he has provided the reader with valuable insights into defining the problems, dealing with stakeholders, developing analyses and recommendations, and modeling philosophy in general."

Thomas B. Sheridan, PhD,
Professor of Mechanical Engineering and Applied Psychology Emeritus,
MIT, USA

"Bill Rouse applies an engineer modeler's questions and tools to help stakeholders identify intrinsic and extrinsic factors that will determine the outcomes of their decisions. This extraordinary book combines a warm personal story of his professional evolution with memorable case examples and pithy lessons. His insights bridge the disciplines of human-centered design, economics, sociology and policy; and span sectors of health care, education, energy and security. It is a must read for anyone interested in tackling large scale change, whether at the level of an enterprise or society."

William W. Stead, MD
McKesson Foundation Professor of Biomedical,
Informatics and Medicine,
Chief Strategy Officer (ret), Vanderbilt University Medical Center

"Thanks to my friendship with Professor Rouse, I have heard numerous snippets of what is in this book over countless lunches and dinners – however, for the first time, this book provides a complete story and context of his evolution from a kid in Rhode Island to a doctoral student at MIT, and then an academic leader at some of the top universities in the US and a member of the National Academy of Engineering. Furthermore, while many may share a variation on his life story – tinkering with toys, tools, and cars, and then evolving into a stellar career in engineering – very few take the time to provide an easily accessible narrative along with priceless insights and reflections. This book is a joy to read, and I believe would be an inspirational guide to many middle and high school kids. This should be on the reading list of all school counselors and parents. I enjoyed reading this!"

Dinesh Verma, PhD
Professor, School of Systems & Enterprises (SSE),
Executive Director, Systems Engineering Research Center,
Executive Director, Acquisition Innovation Research Center

Bigger Pictures for Innovation

This book comprises a set of stories about being an engineer for many decades and the lessons the author learned from research and practice. These lessons focus on people and organizations, often enabled by technology. The settings range from airplanes, power plants, and communication networks to ecosystems that enable education, healthcare, and transportation. All of these settings are laced with behavioral and social phenomena that need to be understood and influenced.

The author's work in these domains has often led to the question: "Well, why does it work like that?" He invariably sought to understand the bigger picture to find the sources of requirements, constraints, norms, and values. He wanted to understand what could be changed, albeit often with much effort to overcome resistance.

He found that higher levels of an ecosystem often provide the resources and dictate the constraints imposed on lower levels. These prescriptions are not just commands. They also reflect values and cultural norms. Thus, the answers to my question were not just technical and economic. Often, the answers reflected eons of social and political priorities. The endeavors related in the book often involved addressing emerging realities rather than just the status quo. This book is an ongoing discovery of these bigger pictures.

The stories and the lessons related in this book provide useful perspectives on change. The understanding of people and organizations that emerges from these lessons can help to enable transformative change. Fundamental change is an intensely human-centric endeavor, not just for the people and organizations aspiring to change, but also for the people helping them. You will meet many of these people in this book as the stories unfold.

The genesis of this book originated in a decision made early in the author's career. He had developed a habit of asking at the end of each day, "What did I really accomplish today?" This was sometimes frustrating as he was not sure the day had yielded any significant accomplishments. One day it dawned on him that this was the wrong question – He needed to ask, "What did I learn today?" It is always possible to learn, most recently about public health and climate change.

In planning this book, the author first thought in terms of accomplishments such as projects conducted, systems built, and articles and books published. He could not imagine this being interesting to readers. Then, it struck him – It is much more interesting to report on what he learned about people and organizations, including how he helped them accomplish their goals. This is a book of stories about how these lessons emerged.

Bigger Pictures
for Innovation

Creating Solutions,
Managing Enterprises,
and Influencing Policies

William B. Rouse

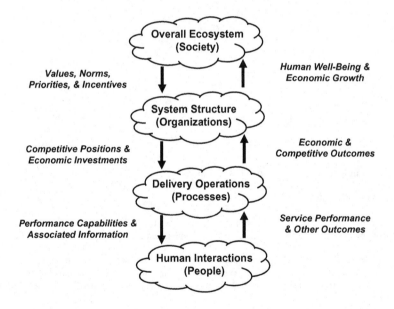

Routledge
Taylor & Francis Group

A PRODUCTIVITY PRESS BOOK

First published 2023
by Routledge
605 Third Avenue, New York, NY 10158

and by Routledge
4 Park Square, Milton Park, Abingdon, Oxon, OX14 4RN

Routledge is an imprint of the Taylor & Francis Group, an informa business

ISBN: 978-1-032-43056-0 (hbk)
ISBN: 978-1-032-43055-3 (pbk)
ISBN: 978-1-003-36554-9 (ebk)

DOI: 10.4324/9781003365549

Typeset in Minion
by Deanta Global Publishing Services, Chennai, India

Dedicated to

Rebecca and Will

Contents

Preface

This book is a set of stories about being an engineer for many decades and the lessons I learned from research and practice. These lessons focus on people and organizations, often enabled by technology. The settings range from airplanes, power plants, and communication networks to ecosystems that enable education, healthcare, and transportation. All of these settings are laced with behavioral and social phenomena that need to be understood and influenced.

My work in these domains has often led me to ask, "Well, why does it work like that?" I invariably sought to understand the bigger picture to find the sources of requirements, constraints, norms, and values. I wanted to understand what could be changed, albeit often with much effort to overcome resistance.

I found that higher levels of an ecosystem often provide the resources and dictate the constraints imposed on lower levels. These prescriptions are not just commands. They also reflect values and cultural norms. Thus, the answers to my question were not just technical and economic. Often, the answers reflected eons of social and political priorities. The endeavors I relate here often involved addressing emerging realities rather than just the status quo. This book is about my ongoing discovery of these bigger pictures.

The stories and the lessons related in this book provide useful perspectives on change. The understanding of people and organizations that emerges from these lessons can help enable transformative change. Fundamental change is an intensely human-centric endeavor, not just for the people and organizations aspiring to change but also for the people helping them. You will meet many of these people in this book as these stories unfold.

The genesis of this book originated in a decision made early in my career. I had developed a habit of asking myself at the end of each day, "What did I really accomplish today?" This was sometimes frustrating as I was not sure the day had yielded any significant accomplishments. One day it dawned on me that this was the wrong question. I needed to ask, "What did I learn today?" It is always possible to learn, most recently about public health and climate change.

In planning this book, I first thought in terms of accomplishments such as projects conducted, systems built, and articles and books published. I could not imagine this being interesting to readers. Then, it struck me. It is much more interesting to report on what I learned about people and organizations, including how I helped them accomplish their goals. This is a book of stories about how these lessons emerged.

William B. Rouse
Washington, DC
July 2022

About the Author

William B. Rouse is Research Professor in the McCourt School of Public Policy at Georgetown University and Professor Emeritus and former Chair of the School of Industrial and Systems Engineering at the Georgia Institute of Technology, USA. His research focuses on mathematical and computational modeling for policy design and analysis in complex public–private systems, with particular emphasis on healthcare, education, transportation, energy, and national security. He is a member of the National Academy of Engineering and a fellow of IEEE, INCOSE, INFORMS, and HFES. His recent books include *Transforming Public–Private Ecosystems* (Oxford, 2023), *Failure Management* (Oxford, 2021), and *Computing Possible Futures* (Oxford, 2019). Rouse lives in Washington, DC.

1

Introduction and Overview

PORTSMOUTH

I was born on January 20, 1947, at Saint Anne's Hospital, in Fall River, MA. Saint Anne's was about 9 miles northeast of our home at 15 Usher Court on Bristol Ferry Road in Portsmouth, RI. This was the road to the ferry to Bristol, RI, across Narragansett Bay. The ferry ceased service when the Mt Hope bridge was opened in 1929.

Portsmouth was founded on the northern end of Aquidneck Island in 1638 by Anne Hutchinson with compatriots John Clarke and William Coddington, all of whom had been banished from the Massachusetts Bay Colony for not conforming to Puritan doctrines. They took boats across the Sakonnet River to land on Aquidneck Island. Rhode Island became a haven for such folks.

Two years earlier in 1636, Roger Williams, banished as well, had founded Providence Plantations on the mainland. One year later, in 1639, Newport was founded on the southern end of Aquidneck Island. Over 100 years later, in 1743, Middletown was founded between Newport and Portsmouth. I have often wondered if a more creative name could have been chosen. Of course, "new port" and "ports mouth" are not particularly creative choices either.

Anne Hutchinson, Roger Williams, and others came together to form the colony of Rhode Island and Providence Plantations. Rhode Island was the colonists' name for Aquidneck Island, the native Americans' name for the island. The colony was one of the most liberal colonies, the home of the first Baptist church, the first Jewish synagogue, and one of the first Quaker meetinghouses.

DOI: 10.4324/9781003365549-1

USHER COURT

Our home, 15 Usher Court, was about 9 miles north of Newport Hospital in Newport, RI. Thus, I could have been born in RI rather than MA. However, my mother, Barbara, was a patient of Dr. James Lent in Tiverton, and his admitting privileges were at St. Anne's. We also did our shopping more often in Fall River. It was more than twice the size of Newport and had many discount stores. Barbara was always looking for a bargain.

Usher Court was a low-income neighborhood with mostly Portuguese immigrants as residents. It included ten houses and several trailers. The houses were built and owned by Raymond Usher, father-in-law of my uncle Jack. Our small house did not have central heat or potable water. One year, my mother let me have the Christmas tree in my bedroom in a large tub. The water in the tub froze solid. As I recall, the rent was $15 per month.

Our heat came from a wood stove in the basement and a kerosene stove in the kitchen. Whenever there was a hurricane or major storm, the town would dump the damaged tree limbs in our yard, which we cut up for firewood. Weyerhaeuser had a facility on the west shore of the island on Narragansett Bay. Freight ships with rough-cut lumber would dock at this finishing facility. The finished wood was delivered to lumber yards such as O'Connell's in Newport and Humphrey's in Tiverton.

Eddie, Joe's brother, worked at Weyerhaeuser. He would bring truckloads of waste lumber pieces, at no charge, and dump them in our yard for our wood stove. Until these odd-shaped pieces were needed for the stove, I was free to build whatever I wanted. I created child-size sports cars and pickup trucks. The neighborhood friends joined me in fantasies using these vehicles. When my mother needed the wood, I would disassemble my creations, carefully removing the nails and straightening them to avoid having to buy new ones.

We did not have a television until Joe and Becky gave us their old TV. Before then, I went next door to Ted and Lillian Shore's to watch *Superman*. As there were no Shore children, they liked having me as a young guest each weekday in the early evening. Once we got our own small black-and-white TV, my mother and I both enjoyed back-to-back Saturday night westerns with Richard Boone in *Have Gun – Will Travel* and James Arness in *Gunsmoke*.

We did not have a car and relied on the Short Line bus service on the west side of the island. I can remember being a six-year-old waiting for the bus from Providence on Bristol Ferry Road to take me to Chase's Farm, halfway down the island, to visit Joe and Becky. It cost one dollar. It is difficult to imagine a six-year-old child having that freedom now. My grandmother, Marian Peirce, also helped us with transportation.

ECONOMY

The population of Portsmouth in 1947 was roughly 5,700 people. There were no major employers until Raytheon moved its Submarine Signal Division to Portsmouth in 1959 to be close to the US Navy in Newport, its major customer. This Raytheon Division plays a major role in my stories in Chapter 2, on being an engineering assistant at Raytheon from 1967–69.

The Newport Naval Station was the predominant employer in Newport, with well over 10,000 employees. General Electric (GE) was a significant employer – my mother was an employee – but GE relocated several decades ago because of high taxes and strong unions. The Naval Station and Raytheon are still the major employers on the island, although tourism is also a major component of the economy.

Portsmouth, during my childhood, was a bedroom town for Newport, Fall River, and Providence, as well as an agricultural economy for corn, potatoes, tomatoes, and a wide range of produce. Our home at Usher Court included potato fields on three sides and Bristol Ferry Road to the west. Anne Hutchinson elementary school was across the street. My first six grades of schooling occurred there.

ROLE MODELS

My mother's side of the family was all nearby. Uncle Joe managed a large produce farm, Chase Farms, in Portsmouth. Uncle Norm was head of maintenance for the Berkshire Hathaway textile plants in Fall River. Aunt Nancy was the Portsmouth reporter for the Newport Daily News. Uncle Jack was head of maintenance for the Rumford Chemical plant in East

Providence. Uncle Bill ran a drywalling business on Cape Cod. Aunt Laura operated a yarn shop on Cape Cod.

No one in my mother's generation went to college, despite several of their parents and grandparents having attended college. The Great Depression, the 1938 Hurricane, and World War II broke this pattern. People just tried to get by and hope that nothing else would go wrong. They referred to this as having a "depression mentality." It stayed with them for the rest of their lives.

My father, who divorced my mother when I was quite young, was a photographer, mainly of baby pictures. He later formed a company focused on fire alarms and residential security with operations in MA and RI. Thus, everyone I knew was a skilled tradesman or small businessman. No one had gone to college. These were my role models as I entered my teenage years.

SMALL BUSINESSES

I became a tradesman and small business owner. I first worked for uncle Joe's plumbing company and another man's painting company. Soon, I had my own business, taking care of 12 families' yards, mowing grass, tending gardens, and many odd jobs. I started painting houses, exterior and interior. By the late 1950s and early 1960s, I was earning about $100 per month. I could buy my own clothes, which was a relief to my mother.

I decided to start an egg business and needed a chicken coop. I asked our landlord at 289 Freeborn Street if I could resurrect the ramshackle remains of a garage on the edge of our property to create a new building. She told me to do whatever I thought was necessary as the building in its current state of condition was of no use to anyone.

I placed a tall ladder on the middle of the side of the garage, climbed to the roof, punched a hole at the ridgepole, and used a handsaw to saw the garage in half, moving to the other side once I had completed the first. When I finished the second half, the front of the garage collapsed. I then took several days to use the wood from the collapsed half to rebuild the remaining half into a serviceable building.

Next, I transformed the building into a chicken coop, with a raised floor. The bottom side of the floor was covered in wire to discourage foxes. I acquired two dozen Rhode Island Reds, and once they had matured, I became the egg supplier to my extended family. The egg business lasted two to three years until the chickens were past their egg-laying prime, when I sold the whole flock.

At age 14 in 1961, I bought my first car, a 1953 Plymouth Belvedere for $35. I taught myself to drive in the field behind our then-home at 289 Freeborn Street. I created a circular track without realizing it, learning about it when a picture of an aerial survey of the town was published in the local newspaper. I could only make left turns and never got beyond second gear, but I learned how to drive.

Using only dirt roads through farm fields, I could drive from our house to Portsmouth's downtown, without ever being on a public road. Downtown included a gas station, grocery store, liquor store, diner, and antique store. This drive through the fields was very rough on the car. At one point, I had to rebuild the carburetor. I could not afford the parts, so I used pieces from my Erector Set to jerry rig the linkages I needed. It worked.

I started another business once I had my license. I would borrow my uncle's 1950 Dodge pickup truck and remove old junk cars from people's yards. I did not pay them or charge them but sold parts from these cars and took the carcasses to Tony Roche's junkyard. Taking things apart, I learned a lot about how things seemed to work. Between this activity and my stints installing and repairing plumbing and heating systems, my interests in mechanical engineering emerged.

OTHER ROLE MODELS

As I contemplated college, my mother informed me I would have to pay for myself. I thought about majoring in business as all my role models were working in businesses or running their own businesses. However, my mother provided me with stories of two alternative, compelling role models. These stories helped me to see that there were alternatives other than being a small business entrepreneur. I return to this in Chapters 5 and 6.

My mother's grandfather was Charles Carrol Peirce. He attended MIT for two years (1882–84) before he was lured away to first join the Fall River Line and then General Electric, which had just been formed by

J.P. Morgan orchestrating the merger of Edison Electric and Thomson-Houston Electric Company in 1892. He became an executive in the railway division of GE and led the electrification of the first railway in the USA, the Nantasket Line. He chaired the alumni celebration of MIT, moving to Cambridge in 1916.

His father was George Patton Peirce, a legendary builder of passenger ships for routes between Boston and New York City. His best-known ships were the Fall River Line's Puritan, Pilgrim, Providence, and Priscilla, which was called the Queen of Long Island Sound. His ships were elegant, luxurious, and on the leading edge of technology. His son, Charles, led the electrification of the ships, eliminating the kerosene lamps that often led to ship fires.

My mother told me family stories of Charles and George. The stories of Charles were not always flattering. It became very clear to me that there were many more interesting possible futures than operating a small business in Portsmouth, RI. Boston was the shining city on the hill, but I was not sure how to get there. However, it became clear that the path involved engineering – in my case, mechanical engineering, due to my deep involvement in cars and plumbing.

HIGH SCHOOL AND COLLEGE

I was not a good student in high school, despite somehow qualifying for the National Honor Society. I devoted my energies to making money and any car deals I could pull off. I was achieving a C in high school math, while I achieved the highest math SAT score in Middletown High. I enjoyed the wood shop and foundry. My favorite course was economic geography. There was so much more on my agenda than high school.

I applied to the University of Rhode Island (URI) and Brown University and was accepted at the former and rejected by the latter. As I was paying for college myself, URI was my only realistic alternative, so there was no angst over Brown. I remember the first day at URI when we were told, "Look to your left. Look to your right. Only one of the three of you will be here next year." That's what happened.

In my freshman year, I earned two C grades: one in chemistry and one in physical education. I strongly disliked chemistry, in part due to the

500 student lectures. Chemistry labs were such that you took one white liquid and mixed it with another white liquid, the result being a third white liquid. I needed more visual feedback than that. Chemistry was not something you appreciated; it was something you got over.

When I started engineering, electrical engineering was, by far, the most popular engineering major. I chose mechanical engineering. You can see gears and shafts. You cannot see electrons. I have a strong need to visualize phenomena of interest. I cannot relate to reality purely as an abstraction. Perhaps that is why I found chemistry so daunting. However, my sense of understandable abstractions has substantially evolved, as illustrated in later chapters.

BECOMING AN ENGINEER

My approach to school was transformed by my sophomore year in mechanical engineering at URI. I learned to studiously do my homework. For my engineering classes, this meant solving homework problems. When I developed a deep understanding of how to formulate and solve various classes of problems, for example, in kinematics or dynamics, I was able to do very well in my exams, earning A grades in almost all of my classes.

I needed a different approach for classes such as western civilization. Exams depended on having memorized people, places, dates, etc. I have good memory skills, as evidenced by my abilities to remember all the names of my elementary school teachers and the names of all the mechanical engineering faculty members – many decades after interacting with them. However, memorization is not one of my preferred ways to learn.

I prefer to understand first principles, e.g., conservation and continuity, and employ these principles to formulate problems. I can then solve the representations of formulations using a wide range of mathematical tools. In the real world, rather than the classroom, I can then compare these solutions to actual data on the phenomena of interest. If such comparisons are not favorable, I revisit the formulation of the problems.

After my freshman year at URI, I spent the summer working for my uncle Joe's plumbing company. Portsmouth had recently installed city water mains. Homeowners had to hire plumbers to connect their houses to the mains. This involved digging ditches from streets to homes, laying copper pipes from the street to the basement, and connecting these pipes to the water systems in the homes.

Joe contracted with Eddie de Arruda to use his backhoe to dig the ditches. My job was in the ditches, smoothing and leveling the surfaces of the bottoms of the ditches upon which the pipes would lay. It was hot, sweaty, physical work, but I enjoyed being part of our three-person team.

One day, as we were taking a break, Eddie commented, "You know, Bill, with your engineering education, you will someday be sitting in an air-conditioned office and wondering about whether those poor sons of bitches, Joe and Eddie, are still digging ditches out in the blazing sun." We all had a good laugh.

He was completely correct. Following my sophomore year, I obtained an internship at Raytheon, thanks to Alan Wyant, the vice president for product assurance at the Submarine Signal Division on West Main Road in Portsmouth. Alan knew me from the Community Methodist Church, which we both attended. His daughter was my age. In contrast to many current practices, this internship was very well paid. I worked for Raytheon for the next two years, gaining experiences discussed in Chapter 2.

As graduation from URI approached, I interviewed with several companies. I received attractive offers from Raytheon as well as GE, IBM, and US Steel. In parallel, I applied to graduate school at URI, RPI, and MIT. All three accepted me. I was shocked by the MIT's acceptance. My mother was thrilled. I would be following in the footsteps of her grandfather to MIT, albeit almost 90 years later.

My decision hinged on traveling to MIT and obtaining a research assistantship to pay my tuition and living costs. I had gained two primary interests at URI – system dynamics and control, and materials science. The former interest was furthered by my two years at Raytheon, while the latter was simply based on coursework. I interviewed one professor in each area. Both offered me assistantships.

I accepted the offer from Tom Sheridan. I would major in system dynamics and controls, working on a NASA grant. Tom headed the human–machine systems laboratory. The focus was on the roles and performance of humans in complex systems. My MS thesis and PhD dissertation centered on humans' performance in air traffic control. What I learned from this research is discussed in Chapter 2.

BUSINESS EXPERIENCES

Based on the environment where I grew up and my available role models, I started service businesses in yard care and home painting, and product businesses selling eggs and used car parts. All of these were commodity businesses. The same services and products were widely available from other vendors. My only competitive advantages were my past performance and my family-based relationship network.

However, even from these fledgling businesses, I learned some core principles. First, you have to sell the service or product before you get to deliver the service or product. So delivering the work depends on selling the work. Simply being good at the work was not sufficient.

Second, reference customers, who were pleased with what they bought from you, can motivate new prospects to try your offerings. Better, yet, if references and prospects work for the same company, have social connections, and are professionally affiliated or perhaps physical neighbors.

Finally, pay careful attention to social networks, not just Facebook or Twitter, which, of course, did not exist then, but through schools, sports, churches, and other social "clubs." Such connections can help you to succeed and help you to get your wonderful technology into the market.

Over 25 years later, I founded several companies that intended to yield more than my personal income. This required more than an occasional extra pair of hands. We had to grow the staff, provide benefits, and create career growth paths. These later business ventures, discussed at length in later chapters, were three technology companies (mainly software): Search Technology, Inc. (1980), Search Aeronautics (1985), and Enterprise Support Systems, Inc. (1990), and two consulting companies, Rouse Associates, LLC (2001), and Curis Meditor, LLC (2017).

The value proposition of these companies involved a central principle. Customers might not decide to buy from us, but they could not get what we offered elsewhere in terms of software systems and tools, as well as associated expertise. Certainly, they could find other ways of meeting their needs, but our technology and expertise were designed to be uniquely appealing and cost effective.

The principles outlined above reminded me of an experience I had as CEO of Search Technology. A group of young engineer employees wanted to meet with me. They asked, "If our offerings are so great, why do we need marketing and sales functions?"

I responded, "We have to communicate with customers so they will understand the high quality of our offerings." Their immediate response was, "If that is true, won't the market eventually learn this on its own?"

Sensing that it was going to be difficult to get this group to abandon their position, I said, "Well, that might work if we had one of the world's greatest ideas." They responded with enthusiasm. I then added, "Unfortunately, we don't have any of the world's greatest ideas!"

Within universities, I founded and led research centers at the University of Illinois, two centers at Georgia Tech, and another at Stevens Institute, as well as chairing the Industrial Engineering Division at Illinois and the School of Industrial and Systems Engineering at Georgia Tech. Not surprisingly, these endeavors had similar research content to my companies, but they did not have the zeal to put solutions into the marketplace. I wanted to create things that had impacts.

My two years at Raytheon were the only time I was employed by a large corporation, learning about reporting structures, career ladders, and office politics. Fortunately, my customers and clients have included over 100 major corporations, agencies, and non-profits. Thus, I have experienced extensive interactions with CEOs, COOs, CFOs, CTOs, etc. Consequently, the perspectives presented throughout this book are very broadly based.

TRANSITIONS TO BIGGER PICTURES

These opportunities and my decisions fundamentally shaped the journey and stories I relate in this book. As discussed in Chapters 2–4, my journey for the next two decades involved applying my systems science and engineering models to complex systems where behavioral and social phenomena played central roles. This ranged from operations and maintenance of complex engineered systems to, more recently, healthcare, higher education, and urban and environmental systems. This research drew upon a well-defined set of modeling paradigms applied to a broad set of behavioral and social phenomena.

The above work focused on technology for training and aiding operators and maintainers of complex engineered systems. During the subsequent two decades, as discussed in Chapters 5–7, sponsors and clients' interests evolved to seek help for new product planning and strategic management more broadly. This led me to encounter organizational, social, and cultural phenomena that sometimes dominated technical and economic issues. We needed to address organizational needs and beliefs, as well as strategic assumptions and delusions that threatened to thwart enterprise success. The formation of several of my companies was due to opportunities to support change processes.

Over the past decade, the scope of my research expanded to address complex ecosystems rather than individual enterprises and markets, as discussed in Chapters 8–10. This culminated in researching complexity and change across technologies, organizations, and society in domains such as national security, healthcare delivery, higher education, and energy and climate. This work has been quite challenging as changing complex ecosystems can be characterized as "wicked problems," involving strongly vested interests with legacy investments whose value they aggressively seek to sustain.

I want to emphasize that this book is not intended to be simply a chronology of my positions, companies, institutions, and accomplishments. In contrast, this three-phase journey provides a scaffolding for a wealth of lessons learned. These lessons are discussed in the last two chapters of the book.

DESIGN, MANAGEMENT, AND POLICY

There are a range of lessons about design, management, and policy, which are discussed in Chapter 11. Over the past three decades, I have refined and extended the construct of human-centered design, a process of considering and balancing the values, concerns, and perceptions of all the humans involved in designing, developing, acquiring, operating, and maintaining a product, service, or system. Committed use of human-centered design can identify tradeoffs, conflicts, and viable paths forward.

Key stakeholders play central roles. Identifying and communicating with these stakeholders is essential for success, including addressing tradeoffs with their explicit involvement. Sometimes, resolving tradeoffs requires expanding the "trade space" to include issues and opportunities beyond the design effort of interest. In particular, providing a reluctant stakeholder with a "win" on an unrelated issue may cause them to accept a bit of a "loss" for the design solution at hand.

Computational models for exploring tradeoffs should represent the levels of abstraction and aggregation that interact to affect outcomes. People interact with processes that result from organizations' investments, in the context of societal priorities, incentives, values, and norms. It is very difficult to make changes at one level without considering the impacts of the other levels.

Interactive visualizations of computational models can greatly enhance stakeholders' engagement, particularly for those without technical backgrounds. Policymakers, for example, would like to embrace evidence-based decision making but may be unfamiliar with the necessary analytics. Interactive visualizations can enable them to explore assumptions and scenarios without dealing with the underlying mathematics.

The complexity of the technical, organizational, social, and societal ecosystems associated with designing solutions can be daunting, whether they are embodied in hardware, software, or policy. Understanding the nature of complexity, and how it is manifested in the context of interest, can be crucial to avoiding very reasonable solutions that are really bad ideas. The goal is to get rid of bad ideas quickly.

Overall, stakeholder involvement is essential. The goal should be the alignment of incentives, with transparent tradeoffs explored from multiple perspectives. Long-term ambitious aspirations should be balanced with near-term early, albeit often small, wins that sustain the confidence of key stakeholders. Waiting too long for anything tangible to happen typically undermines support.

Learning and leveraging these lessons involved forming and working with multi-disciplinary teams of engineers, economists, behavioral and social scientists, and other disciplines. This was required because the phenomena underlying the multi-level formulations of problems included physical, human, economic, and social phenomena. This ranged from the physics of the problem, to the human elements at each level, to the economics of the "as is" and "to be" system, and to the social context, values, and norms overarching everything.

PUBLIC–PRIVATE ECOSYSTEMS

Lessons about public–private ecosystems include those learned regarding national security, healthcare delivery, higher education, and energy and climate. These lessons are also discussed in Chapter 11. Changes in these ecosystems are very difficult and require flexible applications of the lessons learned in design, management, and policy.

National security involves the largest organization in the world. It is well resourced. However, overwhelming organizational inertia and pervasive risk aversion make it difficult to get new ideas and technologies adopted. Performance, schedule, and cost challenges receive intense scrutiny. Technological dominance has been waning, with most innovations emerging from the commercial sector.

In healthcare delivery, the science of medicine dominates the science of healthcare delivery. Innovations in delivery are difficult to scale to broader success due to a lack of portable leadership. In the USA, fragmentation of providers and payers seriously undermines the quality of care. The pandemic has prompted significant change, for example, in telemedicine. Overall, technological disruption is underway, particularly via data analytics and artificial intelligence.

Higher education's traditions of guilds (disciplines) dominate curricula, hiring, promotion, and tenure. The organizational model that originated in Bologna in 1088 is still strong, i.e., colleges, schools, and departments. Tuition increases have outstripped inflation due to the strong growth of non-faculty costs. Foreign student "cash cows" are diminished due to the parity of other countries' institutions and US immigration challenges. Technological disruption is underway, particularly via online delivery.

The energy and climate ecosystem involves strong vested industry and political interests, enabled by the durable energy consumption habits of everyone. Needs for change are increasingly recognized widely. Maturing technologies, i.e., hydro, solar, wind, and next-generation nuclear, are much less expensive and more climate friendly. A major challenge is the delivery infrastructure, which is highly fragmented and fragile.

CONCLUSIONS

This chapter has briefly outlined the roots of my aspirations to create solutions, manage enterprises, and influence policies. My journey has involved numerous episodes of problem formulation and analysis, solution synthesis and construction, and, in several instances, founding and managing enterprises to bring solutions to markets. There were a few major successes, many minor successes, and, admittedly, a few fizzles.

This book might be read as a report on the formation and execution of a grand plan. That was not the case. Instead, my strategy was to place myself in the path of serendipity or, better yet, at the crossroads of serendipity. My agenda aligned with others' agendas sufficiently often to enable significant progress. Relationships were key factors in success.

Many years ago, I mentioned to my colleagues at Georgia Tech that I always seem to do my most creative work when I am at the edge of incompetence. They reacted quite negatively, saying they would never allow themselves to be in that position. However, not being sure of what you are doing, and seeking to figure things out, results in enormous learning. Some of this learning involves exploring and understanding bigger pictures.

2

Human Behavior and Performance

PROLOGUE

My undergraduate education in mechanical engineering, as well as my work at Raytheon, involved the mathematical modeling of physical systems. Humans may have operated or maintained these systems. However, the equations of my models did not include humans. It was not until MIT, discussed in this chapter, that I expanded my purview to consider human–machine systems. Now, the equations had to include representations of human behaviors. I also had to consider humans' abilities and limitations in terms of the extent to which they could behave as needed. This led me to explore human anthropometry, physiology, and psychology. Sociology would come later.

INTRODUCTION

In this chapter, I relate experiences associated with understanding and supporting human behavior and performance. Behavior is what people do – the actions they take, such as control actions (e.g., steering) or selection of actions (e.g., accessing a display). Performance is how well they do, typically defined in terms of task-specific metrics related to accuracy and speed.

The humans discussed in this chapter are professionals performing work-related tasks. They are operators, maintainers, designers, or researchers. I only consider individual performers. Operational teams, design groups, and other social entities are addressed in later chapters. Then, I consider how people work together and address tradeoffs together, and sometimes conflict.

DOI: 10.4324/9781003365549-2

RAYTHEON

My first exposure to people who operate complex systems was as an engineering assistant at Raytheon. My assignment was to determine the optimal provisioning of spare parts for sonar systems on submarines. This is very much complicated by the limited space for spare parts on a submarine.

Maintainers on submarines have to deal with two problems – the mean time between failures of components and the mean time to repair failures. The overarching concern is system availability, which equals uptime divided by uptime plus downtime. They are not only concerned with the means, or averages, but also the full probability distributions of times to failure and repair.

The inventory of spare parts greatly affects availability. Parts that fail often require many more spares than those that rarely fail. Parts that can be repaired onboard require fewer spares. I developed a computer program that simulated the random occurrence of failures and subsequent maintenance to predict the probability distribution of availability.

Two related efforts were concerned with the design of the sonar system. Sonar systems ping audio signals that are reflected by objects in their path and thereby provide a return signal that is detected and analyzed on the submarine. These pings result in very high G loadings on the cone-shaped Belleville springs that support the pinging mechanism. My task was to analytically predict the stress levels in the springs and assess whether these levels could be sustained without failing. They could.

The calculation of mean time to repair assumes a lognormal distribution of repair times, but test data showed the distribution was bimodal. The first mode – or peak of the distribution – related to electrical repairs which mainly involved removing and replacing the failed part. The second mode related to mechanical repairs, which usually involved actual repair of the failed part rather than just removal and replacement. I was tasked with determining how the mean time to repair should be calculated for bimodal repair times.

The motivation for this request was test data that showed the overall sonar system was not meeting the required mean time to repair. I developed an approach to analyzing this bimodal data and presented it to the maintainability manager. He was very supportive but reported that new test data showed that the system now met the requirement. I emphasized that the calculation was still wrong. He did not disagree but said that was now a moot point.

My two years at Raytheon gave me a wonderful opportunity to exercise my technical skills and gain confidence in my education having provided me with valuable capabilities. It also helped to realize that I did not want to end up focusing on a single spring in an overall complex system. I wanted a broader purview of the bigger picture of the sonar system and submarine.

I learned several lessons about corporate culture. The experience of the maintainability calculation showed me that contractual requirements can trump technical correctness. As I was approaching graduation, Raytheon offered me a full-time position in mechanical engineering. I had spent two years in systems engineering, where my boss, Alec Garnham, wanted to bring me aboard full time. Human resources nixed that because my degree was in mechanical engineering. This made the decision to go to graduate school much easier.

MIT

Air traffic controllers oversee the sequencing of aircraft to land at airports. They do this by monitoring images of the aircraft on computer screens and communicating with the air crews on the planes. The research question for my MS thesis was whether predictor displays could help controllers perform better in terms of spacing aircraft for landing.

A predictor display employs a mathematical model to project the future path of an aircraft based on its current state, i.e., three-dimensional position and velocity. This future state is displayed as the likely future path of the aircraft over the next 10–30 seconds. The research question was how controller performance would be affected by prediction length, i.e., number of seconds, and starting situation, i.e., initial degree of alignment with the desired sequencing.

To address this question, I built an air traffic control (ATC) simulator. The dynamics of three aircraft were simulated on an EAI (Electronic Associates, Inc.) analog computer, as were the projections for the predictions for each aircraft. I designed and built a control station that included the controls for the three aircraft with connections to the EAI computer. The positions of the aircraft were sent to an IBM digital computer for later analysis.

Controllers were the subjects in the experiment, seated in front of the ATC display. They communicated with the pilots via headphones. I played the roles of all three pilots, adjusting the controls to accomplish the controllers' requests. Beyond varying prediction length, three initial conditions were studied: (1) easy with sequence alignment not requiring much change, (2) moderate with considerable alignment change needed, and (3) drastic with aircraft collisions likely without substantial changes.

The results were clear. Predictor displays did not improve performance for the easy initial conditions, improved performance substantially for the moderate conditions, and did not improve performance for the drastic conditions. Controllers addressed the drastic conditions by abandoning the sequencing goal and moving the aircraft far away from each other rather than attempting landing. Prediction lengths of 10–20 seconds helped, but 30 seconds was too long and misleading.

We communicated these practical results to NASA Ames Research Center, the sponsor of our grant and my assistantship. It was a very positive learning experience for me, particularly in terms of getting all the pieces of technology working together. Designing and fabricating the control station helped me to learn aspects of electronics that I had not encountered in my electrical engineering classes.

My PhD dissertation addressed the question of what limits humans from predicting accurately in terms of cognitive sources of suboptimal human prediction. To pursue this question, I abstracted the prediction task to one of simply asking subjects to predict the next state of a displayed sequence, or time series, of system states. They made this prediction by moving a cursor on a computer screen. I then displayed what actually happened. They predicted the next state, and so on.

I programmed this experimental setup on a PDP-8 computer in PAL-8 assembly language. This required an in-depth understanding of the Digital Equipment Corporations' PDP-8. It was introduced in 1965 and costs $18,500–$150,000 in today's dollars. It had 4,096 12-bit words of memory. This amount of computing power is completely dwarfed by contemporary digital devices such as iPhones.

It was a tradition in Tom Sheridan's lab that the most senior graduate student managed the computer. When it became my turn, I discovered that our PDP-8 was No. 50 in eventual sales of over 50,000 computers.

Consequently, the standard technical documentation did not match our computer. Several standard maintenance procedures could not be accomplished on our computer.

Failure diagnosis often had to be accomplished with an analog panel meter, i.e., Simpson meter, to trace sources of disrupted current flow. This resulted in my becoming quite intimate with the innards of the PDP-8. Fortunately, my experiences with automobiles and plumbing that I related in Chapter 1 gave me the confidence to take things apart. I consider my PDP-8 experiences to be an important part of my education.

A central question in this research was what limits prediction accuracy. Addressing this question required a baseline against which to compare human performance. I used stochastic (probabilistic) estimation theory to develop an algorithm that could perform the task that I was asking humans to do. I found that an algorithm with fading memory mimicked human performance quite well over a wide range of conditions, i.e., from highly predictable to very unpredictable time series.

This suggested that humans pay great attention to recent elements of the time series but do not consider earlier elements of the time series. If I had the stochastic estimation algorithm performed without the fading memory, it performed very much better than the human subjects. Interestingly, the predictions of the unconstrained algorithm were what could be used for predictor displays. Hence, I now had a defensible explanation for why predictor displays helped.

Another cognitive source of suboptimal human prediction could be motivation. Perhaps humans are only willing to put in limited effort when performing the prediction task. To test this idea, I converted the experimental task into a game and varied the reward scheme so rewards ranged from linear with accuracy to nonlinear with increasing accuracy. In other words, performing really well led to much greater rewards.

I advertised for subjects and was surprised that MIT undergraduates were anxious to play the game. Many said that they would play without being paid. That was not going to work. I tried other tasks such as doing multiplication tables. MIT students enjoyed this too, offering to do it again without pay to see if they could do better. I tried a task where people did nothing. They just sat in front of a blank screen. Many of them slept.

I finally devised a game with no intrinsic reward. Subjects were asked to memorize X words in the dictionary. One group was paid a fixed amount per correct word. The other group was paid an accelerating amount per correct word. This group averaged more than double the number of correct words. I came to deeply understand the difference between intrinsic and extrinsic rewards.

MIT provided another essential lesson. Midway through my first semester, I had failing grades in all my classes. Although I graduated at the top of my University of Rhode Island (URI) class, I was not sufficiently prepared to compete with all my classmates who had graduated at the top of their classes. I needed to catch up – quickly.

I bought all the relevant undergraduate textbooks for the courses I was failing. I did every homework problem in every book, working late every evening. Put simply, I learned what MIT undergraduates had learned in terms of mathematical representations of phenomena associated with dynamics and controls. By the end of the semester, I earned A grades in all my classes.

TUFTS UNIVERSITY AND US AIR FORCE

I was commissioned as an officer in the US Air Force by MIT ROTC (Reserve Officers' Training Corps) in May 1971. Based on my research on cognitive limitations, I had arranged to serve active duty at the NIH Institute of Mental Health in Bethesda, MD. This plan was derailed by a letter from the Air Force, indicating that I was eligible for the Palace Option. Due to the winddown of the Vietnam War, the Air Force wanted to trim its officer corps. I need only serve on active duty for 90 days at an Air Force base of my choice and then transition to inactive reserves.

This was attractive, but I needed a job. Serendipity intervened. John Kreifeldt of Tufts University's Department of Engineering Design was about to take a one-year sabbatical. He contacted Tom Sheridan to see if any recent PhD graduates might be interested in a one-year position as visiting assistant professor. Tom brought this to my attention. I had never considered an academic career. Tom convinced me that this would be a low-risk experiment.

I joined the faculty at Tufts. The Medical School and Fletcher School of Diplomacy were prominent; the School of Engineering was less so. I taught undergraduate design and graduate human factors and operations research. Teaching was a new experience for me. I enjoyed lecturing, less so homework, exams, and grading. I enjoy communicating with students much more than evaluating them.

I inherited a research project and a graduate student – my first – at Tufts New England Medical Center. The project was concerned with the automatic control of radiotherapy equipment to support clinicians in the precision positioning of radiation beams. This fits within my system's dynamics and controls background but was not a positive experience. The MDs treated me, a newly minted MIT PhD, as a senior technician. It took me 25 years to reengage with healthcare, as discussed in Chapter 8.

Another research effort stemmed from my studies at MIT. My explorations of humans' abilities to perceive statistical properties led to the first of two studies of people's perceptions of the means and standard deviations of time series. I became interested in how people perceive relationships between displayed points of a time series. On a computer display, these points are often connected with straight lines.

I determined that piece-wise continuous functions resulting from polynomial interpolation have unbiased expected values and biased variances. Results of two experiments showed that humans base their perceptions on the piece-wise continuous result of interpolation and thereby transmit the statistical bias. In other words, connecting discrete data points with straight lines causes people to perceive these lines as just as valid as the empirical data points.

I also continued my investigations of operations research for managing university libraries. This is a fairly rich story of how operations research methods can be employed for improving library management. This was my first venture into understanding and improving organizational performance. This is, of course, a strong suit of operations research, which I was now teaching for the first time.

I served my 90 days of active duty at Air Force Cambridge Research Laboratory at Hanscom Field in Bedford, MA, in the summer of 1973. The commander of the lab, his sergeant administrative assistant, and I were the only Air Force personnel in the lab. All others were civilian employees. My supervisor was Charlton Walter, a branch chief, who took me into the computer room, pointed out my impressive capabilities and told me to do whatever I wanted for my 90 days.

The EAI hybrid computer system, i.e., analog plus digital computers, was similar to the system I had used for the ATC experiments at MIT. However, its capabilities were much greater. The only thing lacking was a problem to address. I talked with several researchers and discovered an opportunity to help them with the analysis of atmospheric research data.

They would launch rockets that would sense various parameters at different altitude levels and store this data on analog tapes. Back in the lab, they would take 35-mm slides of these data tracks, project these slides on walls, and then use handheld rulers to measure magnitudes. I programmed the hybrid computer system to become an interactive graphics display, which researchers employed to smooth and analyze their atmospheric data.

This was such a hit that the lab hired me as a consultant after I completed my 90 days of active duty. It struck me that the researchers' smoothing task was similar to the prediction tasks I employed for my PhD studies. I was given permission to conduct a formal experiment on human performance in this smoothing task. I extended my stochastic estimation algorithm to handle both smoothing and prediction.

This was an important step towards a theory of human performance in stochastic estimation tasks. The 1973 paper on prediction, the 1974 paper on smoothing, and the 1976 paper on the perception of statistics came together in the 1977 paper on the overall theory. The result was an integrated mathematical model that provided a principled explanation for all these phenomena.

UNIVERSITY OF ILLINOIS

After one semester at Tufts, I decided that life as a faculty member was attractive, but not at Tufts. I needed to be at a place large enough that I would have colleagues with similar research interests. I sleuthed around a bit and identified a position at the University of Illinois at Urbana-Champaign (U of I). It was in the Department of Mechanical and Industrial Engineering (M&IE).

I sent a letter plus a resume to the department chair, Helmut Korst. He soon responded with an invitation to interview. I remember my first flight to Willard Airport in Champaign. The endless green fields of corn and soybeans were a new experience for me. I also remember touring the immense U of I campus and feeling like I was in a Walt Disney movie.

I started in January 1974. My first teaching assignment was a required senior course in control theory, one of my favorite topics. I taught this course six times in a row. I also taught a graduate course in control theory and developed my own graduate course in human–machine systems. I soon had enough research funding from the Air Force, DoD, NASA, and the State of Illinois that I only had to teach one course per semester.

I soon affiliated with Coordinated Science Laboratory across the street from M&IE. There were strong research groups in control theory and artificial intelligence, with faculty members mainly from electrical engineering and computer science. Beyond library operations research, which I discuss in Chapter 3, I built a research team focused on two topics.

I had become very interested in how humans perform in multi-task situations and how computers might help them to manage multiple tasks. We conducted a variety of flight-related experiments on how people shared attention among tasks. Yee-Yeen Chu developed a priority queuing model of task management that enabled adding a computer as a second server. The artificial intelligence group focused on how to create capable computer assistants.

Thiruvenkatasamy Govindaraj developed an optimal control theory model of how people share attention between continuous control tasks and discrete tasks. Joel Greenstein developed a pattern recognition model of how people detect process failures. These models helped to inform the creation of an approach to computer-aided multi-task decision making, which we were pursuing with the artificial intelligence group with support from the Air Force.

I became intrigued with human problem solving in general, and detection and diagnosis of failures in particular. I created a graphical simulation of networks and studied humans' abilities to find failed nodes. Experiments focused on the impacts of network complexity and time constraints. Various ways of aiding humans in these tasks were developed and evaluated.

It became quite clear that the aiding was also training subjects to be better problem solvers. This led the Army Research Institute to fund training research with trainees at the Institute of Aviation as subjects. In particular, I worked with Ruston Hunt and William Johnson to study the learning and performance of airframe and power plant mechanics. The overarching question was whether computer-based training would lead to improved troubleshooting of live aircraft engines.

Figure 2.1 is the model of human problem solving that resulted. People try to solve problems by initially relying on readily visible state information. If this is unsuccessful, they explore less visible structural information, e.g.,

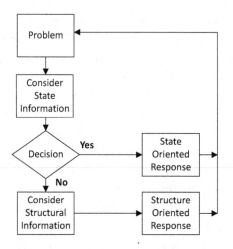

FIGURE 2.1
Model of Human Problem Solving.

what connects to what. The human preferences embodied in Figure 2.1 have an important implication for training and aiding problem solving. I return to this line of research in Chapter 4.

I applied for a sabbatical in 1979–80 and it was approved. My host was the Delft University of Technology, as discussed in the next section. Rather than take the sabbatical, I decided to join the faculty at Delft, mainly because this resulted in a 50% salary increase. This year in Europe led to the conclusion that a permanent move to a large urban setting would be great. Returning to U of I in 1980, now a full professor, I became head of the Industrial Engineering Division. I held this post for one year before my departure to Georgia Tech.

The Illinois experience was, on the whole, wonderful for my career. Being at a top engineering school with many very talented colleagues made for frequent very insightful discussions of phenomena and techniques, ranging from the psychology of multi-task performance to techniques for troubleshooting electrical circuits. I succeeded in making it through the faculty ranks and gaining tenure. I was ready for a new challenge.

DELFT UNIVERSITY OF TECHNOLOGY

First, however, a one-year interlude in the Netherlands provided a new perspective. How did I end up in Delft during 1979–80? Answering this question requires explaining the professional network of researchers studying human behavioral and social phenomena underlying complex systems. This rich network mentored me to become a contributor and colleague with a set of amazing thought leaders.

The Annual Conference on Manual Control began in 1966. I attended the fifth conference at Wright-Patterson Air Force Base in 1970. It was my first conference, and I presented the first paper, having never seen a paper presented. I hosted the 12th conference at U of I in 1976. This community of roughly 100 researchers, many quite eminent, helped me to understand how to present and defend lines of reasoning.

The long-running NATO Conference Series on Human Factors brought together researchers for several days focused on one topic. I participated in four of these conferences over an eight-year period, with conference chairs and locations shown below:

- *Monitoring Behavior and Supervisory Control*, T. Sheridan & G. Johanssen, Berchtesgaden, Germany, 1976.
- *Mental Workload: Its Theory and Measurement*, N. Moray, Mati, Greece, 1977.
- *Human Detection & Diagnosis of System Failures*, J. Rasmussen & W. Rouse, Roskilde, Denmark, 1980.
- *Human Error*, N. Moray & J. Senders, Bellagio, Italy, 1983.

The 1977 conference was where Jens Rasmussen and I first met, although we were aware of each other's work. Sipping drinks around the pool in Mati, the idea for the 1980 conference emerged, resulting in a long collaboration and a 1981 book.

The annual conference of the IEEE Systems, Man, & Cybernetics Society was also a key element of the network. I was president of the society for the two-year (1982–83) period and chaired the annual conference in 1986. Much more recently, the Council of Engineering Systems Universities (CESUN), founded in 2004, has brought together over 50 systems-oriented universities. I served on the CESUN executive committee for ten years and chaired it from 2010 to 2012.

The opportunity to spend a year at the Delft Laboratory for Measurement and Control was due to Henk Stassen's intimate involvement in the professional network just outlined. Tom Sheridan had preceded me as a guest at the lab, so I understood the opportunity. Delft offered me a full-time position, with, as noted, above a 50% increase in salary, so I took a leave of absence rather than a sabbatical from U of I.

Delft was not as focused on aerospace and defense systems. They were much more concerned with process control (e.g., chemical, energy, and power systems). Also located in Delft was TNO (Netherlands Organization for Applied Scientific Research) where I became immersed in supertanker operations, particularly training, which is discussed in Chapter 4.

My year in Europe also involved collaboration with Jens Rasmussen at Riso National Laboratory, in part to organize the NATO Conference on Human Detection and Diagnosis of System Failures. We also intensely studied operator and maintainer performance in nuclear power plants, a top priority of Riso. His deep and creative thinking on this topic continues to influence me.

This period also involved in-depth collaboration with Gunnar Johanssen at FAT (Research Institute for Human Engineering) in Wachtberg-Werthoven in Germany. We studied the planning behaviors of military flight crews in managing aircraft operations. Gunnar subsequently held a one-year visiting position at the University of Illinois and Jens subsequently held a one-year visiting position at Georgia Tech.

The year in Europe was a study in contrast. My collaborations involved studies of human behaviors and performances in process plants, power plants, supertankers, and aircraft. This provided a rich appreciation of how essential phenomena varied across contexts. This understanding has proven to be invaluable for knowing what is generalizable and what depends on context.

GEORGIA TECH: FIRST TIME

By early 1981, I was seriously pursuing opportunities on the east and west coasts. I had formal or informal interviews at Arizona, Berkeley, and Stanford. Mike Thomas, chair of industrial and system engineering at Georgia Tech, called me and asked whether I would consider an opportunity at Tech. I was reluctant. I had never been to Atlanta. He convinced me that it would be worth investing a couple of days.

The visit went well. Mike asked me to send him a letter outlining what I would need to accept a position at Tech. I prepared a five-page, single-spaced letter proposing that I lead a new Center for Human–Machine Systems Research. I requested five other faculty positions, one research staff member, and five graduate students, as well as space, computing infrastructure, and an administrative position. Mike called me in a few days, agreeing to everything, and asking when I would arrive at Tech.

I brought my team from Illinois as well as grants and contracts from the US Army, National Aeronautics & Space Administration (NASA), National Science Foundation (NSF), and Office of Naval Research (ONR). We continued the research portfolio formulated at Illinois. This included computer-aided multi-task decision making, human problem solving in process control (Nancy Morris), computer-aided information retrieval (David Morehead), communications network operations (Richard Henneman), methods for inferring rules underlying human behaviors (Michael Lewis), and methods for inferring operators' intentions (Norman Geddes). Two of these five PhDs were in psychology rather than engineering.

I did not think of it at the time, but the stream of PhD dissertations at Illinois and Georgia Tech were providing pieces for a puzzle that would emerge in 1984 when we joined forces with Lockheed to create an AI-based Pilot's Associate for the Defense Advanced Research Projects Agency (DARPA). We were unique in the sense that we had experimental research results to support the functional design we proposed. I return to this initiative in Chapter 4.

Georgia Tech was different than Illinois. Tech made big bets and committed resources that were much greater than feasible at Illinois. Tech was awash in verbal commitments not supported by written agreements. This concerned me at first, but I soon found that decision makers honored their commitments. Tech had ambitious aspirations, which were realized, and built, on a culture of risk taking and trust. In a second stint at Tech, discussed in Chapter 7, I learned that this culture was greatly affected by the leadership which, of course, changes every decade or so.

CONCLUSIONS

It may not be readily apparent, but all of the studies discussed in this chapter involve four aspects of human behavior and performance:

- Estimation tasks, e.g., prediction, smoothing, filtering.
- Multi-task decision making, e.g., flight management.

- Failure detection and diagnosis, e.g., process control, troubleshooting.
- Information seeking, e.g., researching key documents and findings.

These studies provided insights into the phenomena underlying how humans understand these tasks, behave to execute these tasks, and why particular performance outcomes are achieved. In addition, we devised and evaluated various means to train and aid people to achieve improved outcomes. Training and aiding are discussed in Chapter 4.

This chapter has addressed the behavior and performance of individual operators, maintainers, designers, and researchers. The outcomes achieved are not only affected by individuals' knowledge, skills, and motivation. They are affected by the organizational system within which they operate. More specifically, they are affected by the processes designed to support their behavior and performance.

The next chapter transitions from individual performance to process performance. Thus, to an extent, the emphasis shifts from the people level to the process level. In later chapters, I will add levels for organizations and society. Each additional level enables seeing a bigger picture of how higher levels both enable and constrain lower levels.

EPILOGUE

Herbert Simon observed that the complexity of humans' behavior often reflects the complexity of their environment. In other words, humans adapt to their environment in order to perform acceptably. Driving a car is a good example. If you understand the constraints imposed by the design of the vehicle, roadway, signals, etc., you can predict human driver behaviors because drivers have no choice but to adapt to these constraints.

The structures of the tasks discussed in this chapter dictated people's decisions and behaviors. People had little discretion in making estimates, choosing what to do next, detecting and diagnosing, and information seeking. These constrained tasks did not dictate their exact behaviors, but they only had so much latitude. Thus, modeling their behaviors could begin by modeling the task constraints.

As the stories in this book unfold, the behavioral and social phenomena of interest become less and less constrained. Hence, the people of interest have more discretion. This requires that we know more about human psychology in terms of deciding what to do and executing the chosen tasks. Thus, for example, predicting what cars people will buy is much more difficult than predicting how well they will drive.

FURTHER READING

Rasmussen, J., & Rouse, W.B. (1981). *Human Detection & Diagnosis of System Failures.* New York: Plenum Press.

Rouse, W.B. (1980). *Systems Engineering Models of Human-Machine Interaction.* New York: North-Holland.

Rouse, W.B. (2007). *People & Organizations: Explorations of Human-Centered Design.* New York: Wiley.

Rouse, W.B. (2015). *Modeling and Visualization of Complex Systems and Enterprises: Explorations of Physical, Human, Economic, and Social Phenomena.* New York: Wiley.

Rouse, W.B. (2019). *Computing Possible Futures: Model Based Explorations of "What If?"* Oxford, UK: Oxford University Press.

3

Organizational and Economic Performance

PROLOGUE

Most of my graduate courses at MIT were in my major, system dynamics and control. My minor, by the way, was in history and creative writing. The graduate office policed the choice of minors to ensure that students did not choose topics close to their majors. My choice easily passed muster. I also had to take a language. I chose German. Such requirements have long disappeared.

I also took two courses in operations research (OR) and audited a couple in artificial intelligence (AI). One OR course was with Ralph Keeney, who also was a member of my dissertation committee. It focused on public systems. The other course was on probabilistic modeling, taught by the legendary Alvin Drake. All of my instructors at MIT were first rate.

OR applies analytic methods to support organizational decision making in areas such as capital investments, supply chains, and inventory management. I was interested in moving beyond individual task performance to understand the processes and organizational implications of task performance. For example, how do flows of customers interact with inventories and related services?

The common denominator across all types of organizations is economics. Revenues, costs, and perhaps profits are of concern to management. This is a central topic in industrial and systems engineering. Later in this chapter, I discuss two of my books on this topic, one an edited collection and the other coauthored with Andy Sage.

DOI: 10.4324/9781003365549-3

INTRODUCTION

When I was a graduate student at MIT, the MIT Press conducted an annual book sale with deep discounts on their books. It was held in a large auditorium in the Stratton Student Center. It was there that I encountered Philip Morse's award-winning book *Library Effectiveness: A Systems Approach* (MIT Press, 1968). As my wife Sandra had just completed her MS in Library Science and was employed at the MIT Science Library, I became interested in how operations research (OR) might be applied to library operations.

One of the things that interested me about OR was the emphasis on the operation of real-life systems rather than just mathematical abstractions. This emphasis emerged from people such as Morse immersing themselves in the military needs of World War II. Such works require immersion in the contexts of problems to assure that problem formulations are meaningful and relevant. This emphasis has become seriously diluted in recent decades, with importance shifting to theorems and proofs.

I recall a faculty interview at Illinois where the candidate presented a mathematical model and solution algorithm for determining the optimal values of $x_1, x_2, \ldots, x_N$ for a communications problem. He emphasized the optimization objective and constraints. I asked him what the x values meant physically. He responded, "I do not have the slightest idea." The mechanical engineers in the room later vetoed proceeding with his possible hiring.

More recently at Georgia Tech, I was talking with a young faculty member about collaborating on developing a queuing model of how procurement requests and purchases flow through an organization. We were making slow progress when she told me the context was too complicated. We agreed to abandon the problem. She later dropped by to show me what she was now working on. I commented that you could understand the context of the problem in 60 seconds. She responded, "That's all I am willing to invest."

I firmly believe that engineering valuable solutions to problems requires a deep understanding of the context of the problem in terms of the key stakeholders; their values, concerns, and perceptions; and the avenues and barriers to success. I formalize this notion in terms of human-centered design in Chapter 5.

LIBRARY OPERATIONS RESEARCH

We started quite modestly by studying the staffing of service desks at the MIT Science Library. We collected data on arrival rates and service times. Using standard queuing models, we could project the optimal staffing across times and days to minimize average waiting times for library patrons. This was far from cutting-edge OR, but it clearly showed library managers how better decisions could be made using data rather than intuition.

When we moved to Tufts, we met with the director of libraries and suggested that student teams could help him improve operations. We conducted several studies during the year at Tufts. We generalized our resource allocation formulation to include both human and physical resources. A multi-attribute utility model was developed to proceduralize the decision making associated with selecting sources for acquiring books.

Moving to Illinois, I met with the director of the engineering library to identify interesting projects. One project addressed the dynamics of book circulation, i.e., being checked out by patrons. Using data on past circulation, we developed a model to predict future circulation, which had implications for staffing. We also studied monograph obsolescence, or the process whereby books' circulation approaches zero and can, hence, be remotely archived.

We conducted one study in the Champaign Public Library. Working with architect James Smith, we modeled the flow of patrons among different library services. This had significant implications for where services should be located and which services should be near each other. In particular, this study showed how data on patron flow could inform the redesign of facilities as well as the design of new facilities.

NETWORKED INFORMATION SERVICES

The State of Illinois supports the Illinois Library and Information Network (ILLINET). The purpose of this network is to provide information services to the citizens of the state – all of those with library cards or equivalent. Services range from answering reference questions to providing interlibrary loans.

Service requests are routed through a multi-level network that includes local, regional, and state resources – 3,000 organizations in all. There are 18 regional sub-networks and four major statewide resources. Each regional sub-network can be modeled as a small network with requests for services entering an initial node. Other processing nodes lead to successes that depart from one node, and failures that depart from another node. Failures are routed to other resources for potential fulfillment. Delays and possible service failures are, therefore, encountered at each node.

We developed a queuing network model of ILLINET. This interactive model was used to determine the optimal path through the multi-level network for each type of service. Overall measures of performance included probability of success (P), average time until success (W), and average cost of success (C). Not surprisingly, overall performance is strongly affected by aggregate demands across all services, i.e., the lengths of waiting lines for services affect performance.

The model I developed was purely analytical rather than a simulation. It involved quite a bit of matrix algebra where the matrices reflected network and sub-network structures as well as routing vectors. Parameters within the model included arrival rates for each class of request and service rates for each node in the multi-level network. Data to estimate these parameters came from many thousands of past service requests.

Routes were determined to maximize an overall utility function U (P, W, C) with component utility functions U_P (P), U_W (W), and U_C (C). The relative weights of these component utility functions could be varied, depending on decision makers' preferences. The ILLINET model was used in a variety of ways over several years. Some of these uses surprised us, as we had not anticipated these modes of use. The most memorable application provides a compelling example that illustrates an important lesson learned.

We determined the optimal routing vectors across all types of requests. We found that service could be maintained at current levels for 10% less budget. Alternatively, service (P and W) could be improved without increasing the budget. The key was to avoid one of the largest statewide resource centers, which was very inefficient and expensive. Making this resource center a "last resort" saved a large portion of the 10% but also greatly diminished this resource center's revenue.

A meeting was held in the state capitol in Springfield to discuss this policy. The Director of ILLINET and the Director of the problematic resource center participated, along with other staff members and our team. The ILLINET Director addressed the resource center Director:

> "Do you see what you are costing me?" she asked.
>
> "Yes, I understand but there is not much I can do about it," he responded.
>
> "I know and I am willing to ignore this result, if you will relent on the other issue we have been arguing about for the past several months," she offered.
>
> "Deal. I can do that."

When the meeting ended, I remained to chat with the ILLINET Director.

> "What did you think of the model?" I asked.
>
> "Wonderful. It gave me the leverage to get what I needed," she replied.

This example illustrates the variety of ways in which decision makers employ models. They will seldom just implement the optimal solution. They are much more oriented to looking for insights, in this case, insights that provide leverage in a broader agenda. Models are a means to such ends rather than ends in themselves.

COMMUNICATIONS, MANUFACTURING, AND FAILURE MANAGEMENT

I pursued a variety of studies on the performance of organizational networks. One initiative, with Richard Henneman, focused on monitoring and controlling large-scale networks such as telecommunications networks. We were concerned with hierarchical systems in terms of the number of levels, degree of interconnectedness, and extent of redundancy among nodes. The complexity of such networks was found to relate to both the physical structure of the system and the monitoring and control strategy employed.

The next study addressed enterprise networks for production planning and scheduling. A three-level model was adopted, including planning, scheduling, and operations. The overall architecture that was formulated included five levels for facility-wide situation assessment, facility-wide planning, shop-level situation assessment and workaround planning, normal cell operations, and off-normal cell operations and maintenance.

The result was an integrated approach to addressing both normal and off-normal situations.

Much more recently, I have focused on failure management to address malfunctions of technologies, organizations, and society. Failures are common phenomena in civilization. Things fail and society responds, often very slowly, sometimes inappropriately. What kinds of things go wrong? Why do they go wrong? How do people and organizations react to failures, and what are the best ways to react?

I employed an analytic approach to these questions and addressed 18 well-known cases of high-consequence failures. I employed a multi-level framework to integrate findings across the case studies and, in turn, used these to outline a conceptual approach to integrated failure management.

While the case studies were diverse in terms of their causes and outcomes, my analyses showed that the conceptual design of an integrated approach to failure management could encompass each of the case studies, all of which would have benefited from the same conceptual decision support architecture. This enables cross-cutting system design principles and practices, assuring that failure management in every new domain and context need not start with a blank slate.

Failure management can be effective if we anticipate the types of failures that might occur, develop measures that will enable rapid detection that these failures have occurred, and have proven procedures for accurate diagnoses of what has gone wrong and the implications. Unfortunately, the predominant culture in the USA is to wait until things break and then figure out how to cope with the situation at hand, seldom learning lessons that mitigate subsequent failures. This philosophy has hindered our approach to climate change, as I discuss in Chapter 10.

ECONOMIC MODELING

I gravitated towards teaching courses on engineering-oriented economics. I taught my graduate course on "Understanding and Supporting Human Decision Making" 13 times at Georgia Tech. Similarly, I taught "Advanced Topics in Engineering Economics" 13 times to undergraduate juniors at Stevens Institute. All told, I provided this content to roughly 3,500 students.

My advanced topics course highlighted numerous winners of Nobel Prizes in Economics, including Kenneth Arrow, Herbert Simon, Daniel Kahneman, and Richard Thaler. I invited these luminaries to my class following my expositions of the fundamentals of their contributions. Fortunately, thanks to the wonders of YouTube, they all unknowingly accepted my invitations. This was popular with students.

I spent the summer of 2009 working for the Vice Chief of Staff of the US Air Force. My assignment was to determine how best to project the economic value of investing in people – in other words, valuation of investments in people's training and education, safety and health, and work productivity. The resulting book, *The Economics of Human Systems Integration* (2010), included a variety of theoretical expositions and several case studies.

The overall conclusion was that it is worth investing in the health, safety, and security of people and the public if the organizational entities investing in these benefits are the same entities that gain the returns from these investments. Otherwise, the investing entity sees these expenditures as costs and tries to minimize them.

When I was at Georgia Tech, I served on the Board of Trustees for the Bobby Dodd Institute. Bobby Dodd trained people with disabilities to gain paid employment. They were 100% successful. Consequently, their graduates no longer required Social Security disability benefits. The State of Georgia invested in the training. The federal government received the economic benefits of these investments. Not surprisingly, the state limited the budget for this program.

This fragmentation of organizational players in the USA results in a variety of dysfunctional behaviors. As I discuss in Chapters 8 and 10, the lack of accounting for costs and benefits across organizational levels means, for example, that decreasing healthcare costs is pursued without recognition of the benefits of healthy people working, consuming, and paying taxes.

During this time period, Andrew Sage and I were finishing the second edition of his book *Economic Systems Analysis*. Andy updated the traditional chapters, and I wrote the chapters on advanced topics. I remember reviewing his draft and wading through the mathematics that had once been quite familiar to me. It all held together quite nicely.

I commented to Andy, "This all follows very logically and coherently, but the assumptions you make about human behavior are indefensible."

He responded, "I know the assumptions are ridiculous, but I cannot solve the equations without them." My sense is that one needs to understand these classical economics findings, but behavioral economics provides much better lines of reasoning, as later chapters illustrate.

ORGANIZATIONAL PERFORMANCE

One of my investigations of organizational performance involved one of the companies I founded, Enterprise Support Systems, Inc. (ESS). ESS provided the *Advisor Series* of software tools and associated services, as discussed in Chapter 6. In this section, I discuss my efforts to understand what aspects of the company's processes differentiated successes from failures.

We employed a customer relationship management software application named *Act!* to archive and manage information on our customers, including software tools and services purchased, contact information, histories of exchanges, and even a bit of personal information, e.g., favorite sports teams. Our *Act!* database included roughly 5,000 people.

I used this database to map the ESS relationship network. It became clear that areas of high connectivity in this network were associated with greater sales. High connectivity in any sub-network implies that the people in this sub-network know each other. A straightforward interpretation of this is that satisfied and enthusiastic customers were key elements of our sales force. Customers were helping to sell our products and services to other sales prospects.

This insight prompted me to pursue a very focused strategy of communicating with at least five contacts per day, either face to face, by telephone, or by email. Tracking this for a year resulted in well over 6,000 contacts. This, of course, begs the question of the nature of these communications. Often, I would ask them about their satisfaction with our products and services or check on the status of a pending order.

Many times, we just chatted for a few minutes about their company, competitors, and near-term plans. In the process, I gained a tremendous amount of knowledge about these companies, their markets, and a fair amount of personal information. Recognizing the value of this knowledge, we conducted a small experiment in the late 1990s.

We created an online "article service" for technology-oriented executives and senior managers. This involved reading the top journals in technology management, as well as management more broadly, and identifying articles, or perhaps just illustrations, that we believed would be of great value to particular executives and senior managers.

More specifically, we tracked 30+ journals each week, month, or quarter and identified material relevant to pertinent contemporary issues for 60 targeted executives and senior managers. We then sent them a personal email with this information, with an explanation tailored to their needs. An example was:

> On page 117 of the recent *Harvard Business Review* you will find a table that will help you address the growth-related issue we recently discussed when you present at next week's Board of Directors meeting.

Another example involves an email to a CEO of a home appliance company, "Tom, I see that you are closing the Fort Wayne plant." He responded, "How the hell do you know that?" I replied, "Business Section of the Fort Wayne Journal Gazette this morning." In general, customers were impressed that we were on top of things.

Overall, we sent 500 emails to these 60 managers over an 18-month period. This pilot test was very positively received. Since we had ongoing working relationships with these executives and senior managers, we knew their issues and their information needs very well.

We were well aware that it would be very difficult to scale up this concept for people with whom we did not have ongoing working relationships. Nevertheless, we now knew that it was possible to get managers' benefits/costs right for purposes of information, knowledge, and systems management.

Ongoing evaluation of this offering involved email and telephone interviews and questionnaires. However, the conversion rate from trial to paid subscriptions was an unimpressive 12%. The most frequent reasons identified for non-conversion were:

- The information provided did not match my immediate interests (33%).
- I already have too many information resources (25%).
- I have no means to pay for this type of service (25%).

- Too many free information resources are available to justify paying (17%).

It appeared that these executives and senior managers' time horizons for value were very short. One person told us that the information provided was on target for a meeting tomorrow but that providing it today was of no value. He did not intend to think about the topic at hand until just before he attended the meeting. Many said that they needed exactly the right information at exactly the right time; otherwise, the value of the information plummeted.

Overall, relevance had to be very high and ease of access and use had to be excellent. Willingness to pay for this value was uncertain, although such users have repeatedly demonstrated willingness to pay huge sums for consultants who provide similar information and knowledge. Of course, the associated ease of use of a capable, motivated person who is sitting across the table from you is very difficult to beat.

Much more recently, we have developed a knowledge management platform – www.CurisMeditor.com. This platform provides content aggregation, text analytics, and machine learning to "read" content for users from a corpus of 40 million journal articles and conference papers, as well as 50,000 English language global news articles – per day. My experience has been that this platform enables one to digest hundreds of relevant documents and synthesize actionable insights rather quickly. I elaborate on this in Chapter 4.

Curis Meditor is Latin for health best practices. The overall objective of this platform is to enhance the health of people, processes, organizations, and society. There are dashboards addressing numerous societal challenges, as well as methods and tools for pursuing these challenges. There are online demonstrations of computational tools and descriptions and access to a wide variety of data sets.

We are getting better at addressing organizational needs for access to knowledge and management of knowledge. However, many users present a tough audience. They advocate evidence-based decision making but often rely on gut feelings rather than data. They delegate information seeking to junior colleagues but trump these colleagues' findings with intuitions based on precedence rather than evidence.

Yet, I remain optimistic. The base of data, information, and knowledge continues to grow exponentially. The technology to enable the consumption of this data, information, and knowledge is steadily improving. People are increasingly becoming "digital natives." The crucial need is to continue to cultivate the desire for evidence-based decision making. This is essential to a rational society.

CONCLUSIONS

What did I learn about organizational and economic performance? It was clear that success depends on good people and good processes. Good people and poor processes will yield mediocre performance at best. Hard work helps but cannot compensate for a poorly designed system for product and service delivery.

Thus, success depends on more than the goodness of products and services. Inefficient and ineffective processes will undermine your value propositions. These inefficiencies and remediating quality problems will increase costs and may cause you to raise prices without adding value for customers. This tends to result in losing customers.

Success also depends on the quality of services. ESS had several customers in the UK, including Rolls Royce, Rover, and Royal Ordnance, to name a few. Our Rolls Royce customers were in the aerospace business and located in Newcastle. We were closing in on a significant sale of software tools when the Managing Director asked, "How are you going to service these tools in Newcastle when you are based in Atlanta?"

I responded, "We will guarantee, in writing, any software fixes within 24 hours of you notifying us of problems." That guarantee was written into the contract and the sale was made. Of course, it really helped that any software updates could be emailed rather than hand delivered 6,600 miles away, as the crow flies.

Some time later, this Managing Director was speaking at an industry meeting. He noted our service guarantee and said our quality of service was the best he had ever experienced. This, of course, is exactly what you would like customers to say, especially highly respected and visible customers. These types of outcomes do not happen without well-thought-out and well-executed processes.

The overall lesson is that understanding and supporting your organization is an important key to success. The investments necessary will increase costs, at least initially. However, these fixed costs can be traded off against variable costs which should consequently decrease. More importantly, these investments should result in greater customer satisfaction and thereby increased revenues. With decreased variable costs, these revenues should be more profitable. This can become a virtuous cycle.

EPILOGUE

In this chapter, I have focused on information and economics. These topics intersect when considering the value of information. How much should one be willing to pay to reduce uncertainty? For example, how much would it be worth to be able to determine whether the lottery ticket you are about to buy – *before* you buy it – is a winning ticket? An analytic model can be formulated to determine the value of this tip. If you can get it for less than this amount, it is worth it!

When I was chair of the School of Industrial and Systems Engineering (ISyE) at Georgia Tech, prospective students and their parents often asked, "What is industrial and systems engineering?" After providing various answers that left people confused, I finally found an answer that worked.

If you major in electrical engineering, you will learn about voltage and current. In mechanical engineering, you will pay attention to velocity and acceleration. Civil engineering will teach you about stress and strain. In industrial and systems engineering, our primary concerns are people and money. If you only get to master two variables, we have the best ones.

Mike Thomas recruited me for my first stint at Tech. He was chair of ISyE at the time. He later became Provost. After he stepped down as Provost, the Dean of Engineering, Don Giddens, convinced him to serve as interim chair of biomedical engineering while a national search was conducted for a new chair. A year later, Mike retired from Tech.

At his retirement luncheon, I was asked to make some remarks as I was the current chair of ISyE. I recounted a few stories of Mike's contributions to Tech. Don thanked me and then commented that IE really stood for imaginary engineering. I acknowledged his comments and said that our alumni really appreciated Tech's civil, electrical, and mechanical engineers. This appreciation was reflected by the fact that we employed many of these folks.

The number one ISyE program in the USA, and perhaps the world, at that time had roughly 20,000 alumni. Twenty-five percent of these alumni had job titles of CEO, President, or Partner. They led companies such as AT&T, Berkshire Capital, Delta Air Lines, Dollar General, Interface, Newell Rubbermaid, Reebok, Richway, and Walmart. They employed thousands of engineers, many of them Tech graduates.

I often interacted with many of these executives. One of my favorite questions was, "Do you still feel like an engineer?" Their responses were always something like, "I use my engineering problem solving skills every day."

FURTHER READING

Rouse, W.B. (2007). *People and Organizations: Explorations of Human-Centered Design.* New York: Wiley.

Rouse, W.B. (Ed.). (2010). *The Economics of Human Systems Integration: Valuation of Investments in People's Training and Education, Safety and Health, and Work Productivity.* New York: John Wiley.

Rouse, W.B. (2021). *Failure Management: Malfunctions of Technologies, Organizations, and Society.* Oxford, UK: Oxford University Press.

Rouse, W.B., & Rouse, S.H. (1980). *Management of Library Networks: Policy Analysis, Implementation, and Control.* New York: Wiley.

Sage, A.P., & Rouse, W.B. (2011). *Economic System Analysis and Assessment.* New York: Wiley.

4

Design of Training and Aiding

PROLOGUE

Our studies of human behavior and performance were intended to create and evaluate models that would be of use to designers of complex systems. As I discuss in this chapter, we came to realize that these models could directly benefit operators and maintainers of complex systems via training and/or aiding. This realization was central to our transition to building real products and systems, as I discuss in Chapters 5 and 6.

Succinctly, this transition involved moving beyond studying problems to actually solving them. Of course, studying problems, collecting data, and reporting findings in academic journals is a central activity in academia. That is how you earn promotion and tenure. However, I was finding that my inclinations were more entrepreneurial than scholarly.

I firmly believe that solutions should be evidence based, building upon rigorous research findings. At some point, someone has to take solutions to markets. I could hope that this someone would read my journal articles and then devise strategies and plans for commercializing solutions. Rather than wait for this, I did it myself.

INTRODUCTION

Somewhat simplistically, there are two overall approaches to enhancing humans' behavior and performance. You can enhance their potential to perform via training, or you can directly augment their performance via aiding. Not surprisingly, there are tradeoffs between training and aiding or what we came to term traidoffs. I address this at the end of this chapter.

The design, development, and delivery of training and aiding were the primary value proposition of my first two companies. Search Technology focused on operators, maintainers, and designers, while Enterprise Support Systems addressed designers, managers, and executives.

TRAINING

We had not planned to focus on training. As explained in Chapter 2, we became interested in people's abilities to diagnose the causes of failures in complex networks, for example, the networks associated with information services. We created a computer-generated display of networks and asked people to find the failed node. We provided aiding to show which nodes were, and were not, in the feasible set of failed nodes.

We discovered that the aiding caused people to steadily improve their performance in terms of the number of tests until correct diagnosis. We discovered that we were training people to become better diagnosticians. But, of course, we were only training them to better diagnose failures in context-free networks. The real world is not context free. It is laced with contextual aspects of real-world problems, which are actually the problems that society values being solved.

Our context-free network simulations were labeled, TASK, an acronym for Troubleshooting by Application of Structural Knowledge. Does training via TASK actually improve performance in real-world diagnostic tasks? To address this question, we created FAULT (Framework for Understanding Logical Troubleshooting) which was a context-specific simulation of automotive power plants and aerospace power plants.

We found that training with TASK improved performance in FAULT. However, does either training experience improve performance with live aerospace systems? Our studies found that such training does improve real-life performance. This resulted in extensive publications of our results. Such results can earn one tenure but can they change industry practices?

We formed Search Technology in response to the opportunity to build computer-based training simulators for Marine Safety International (MSI), Inc. MSI asked us if we were ready to do this for real. This opportunity emerged just after my return from a year at the Delft University of Technology where one of my research initiatives at TNO

(Netherlands Organization for Applied Scientific Research) involved training supertanker engineering personnel.

MSI had a very impressive, high-fidelity engine room simulator. Its primary limitation was that it could only accommodate one trainee at a time, as that was the typical staffing practice of the commercial marine industry. MSI wanted a means to productively engage the other members of a typical eight-person class, while one of them was in the full-scope simulator.

Russ Hunt, Bill Johnson, and I addressed this need at the University of Illinois Institute of Aviation for training aviation power plant mechanics. Trainees would engage with live aircraft power plants, but it was not possible to provide each of them with, for example, their own live jet engine. We developed computer-based simulations of aircraft power plants for students to practice with before their turns with the live engines.

MSI contracted with us to design and develop a computer-based simulation of their high-fidelity, full-scope simulator. The moderate fidelity simulator was designed to augment the training of Texaco marine engineers. I traveled to MSI's headquarters at LaGuardia Airport in New York City to demonstrate this new concept to Texaco executives.

The morning did not go well. The executives spent the whole morning criticizing the FAULT-based representation of supertanker propulsion systems. By the time of the lunch break, Gene Guest, President of MSI, said, "We are in trouble. They hate the concept. How can we recover from this terrible first impression?" I told him that I had an idea.

When we reconvened, I told the executives that we were next going to focus on troubleshooting airplane, automotive, and helicopter power plants. These executives were by no means experts on these systems. They quickly came to value how these tutoring systems could help them. A few commented that the problem-solving skills they were learning could easily apply to supertanker power plants. They were now convinced.

The lesson is simple. Never try to convince a domain expert that a low or moderate fidelity simulation of their domain is adequate. Illustrate the concept in a domain where they are not experts. The key point, of course, is that trainees – the target audience – are not yet experts. They need to learn about fundamental phenomena and how to address these phenomena. The experts can no longer relate to being trainees.

We developed and deployed training simulators for a variety of customers, including the Army, Electric Power Research Institute, Duke Power, NASA for the Space Shuttle, and, of course, Marine Safety International. In the process, we formulated the concept of mixed-fidelity training.

The idea was to dovetail low-cost, low-fidelity simulators, e.g., TASK; moderate-cost, medium-fidelity simulators, e.g., FAULT; and expensive, full-scope simulators, such as those used by the airlines and power utilities. There were two primary benefits of this concept:

- One can balance the flow of trainees across each level of simulator, eliminating the bottlenecks of full-scope simulators and thereby enabling larger cohorts of trainees.
- Performance in the full-scope simulators is enhanced if basic knowledge and skills are gained in the lower-fidelity simulators prior to encountering the complexity of the full-scope simulators.

An excellent illustration of these benefits is provided by our application of mixed-fidelity training to crews of the Navy's Aegis Combat System.

THE *VINCENNES* INCIDENT

The Aegis cruiser USS *Vincennes* shot down an Iranian passenger airliner in the Persian Gulf on July 3, 1988. The Aegis weapon system was first commissioned in 1983 with the USS *Ticonderoga*. This system was developed to counter the serious air and missile threat that adversaries posed to US carrier battle groups and other task forces.

The *Vincennes* incident prompted a congressional inquiry. Subsequently, the Office of Naval Research established a research program to study the potential behavioral and social factors underlying this incident. The TADMUS Program was named for its focus – tactical decision making under stress. I was the principal investigator for one subcontractor's efforts in this program.

We studied the crews' training. We reached two conclusions. First, crews were "captured" by their training. Every scenario involved 25 folks facing Armageddon. The Iranian commercial airliner was far from Armageddon, but if that were the only scenario you have ever seen, what would you expect?

The second conclusion concerned teams' mental models. Put simply, teams did not understand what each other was doing and what each team member expected of other team members. If the wide receiver does not expect the quarterback will throw him the ball, team effectiveness can be substantially undermined, not to mention losing the game.

We began by observing teams at the Aegis test facility in Moorestown, New Jersey. This training facility is unusual in that it looks like a ship superstructure rising out of a field west of the New Jersey Turnpike. It is sometimes referred to as the "Cornfield Cruiser."

Training exercises involved 25 people who staff the Combat Information Center (CIC). At the time of our observations, there were typically two exercises per day, each of which took considerable preparation, pre-briefing, execution, and debriefing. Watching these exercises prompted my conclusion that every exercise seemed to be aptly termed "25 folks face Armageddon." This is what Aegis is designed to do. However, as the July 3, 1988, incident shows, not all situations are Armageddon.

We focused our study on the anti-air activities of the CIC, as that is the portion of the team that dealt with the Iranian airliner. Our initial observation of this team suggested that team members did not have shared mental models. In particular, we hypothesized that inadequate shared models of teamwork – in contrast to mental models of equipment functioning or task work – hindered the team's performance.

The overall conclusions of this research were that teams were not well coordinated and did not communicate well in terms of their behaviors in these demanding exercises. It appeared that team members often did not know what was expected of them by other team members and did know what they could expect of others. Without expectations, they did not communicate or communicated erroneously or ambiguously. Occasionally, they could not explain or interpret communications received.

It was clear that these teams needed much-improved shared mental models of teamwork. We developed Team Model Training (TMT), which involved a desktop computer-based training system that approximated the full-scope Aegis simulator. Users of TMT would participate as a member of a team where all other team members were simulated. They would learn their role and, by playing other team members' roles, learn how they fit into the team's performance. They could easily complete 20–30 exercises before venturing into the full-scope simulator.

An evaluation of TMT compared this training with more conventional, lecture-based training. Performance was assessed in the full-scope simulator subsequent to having received one of these training methods.

TMT significantly decreased the overall level of communications, indicating that well-trained teams are not necessarily those with the highest levels of explicit communications. Specifically, frequent requests for clarifications of communications while, for example, addressing missiles incoming in the next few seconds were minimized.

PERFORMING ARTS

I became very interested in the nature of teamwork. My daughter, Rebecca, and I undertook an evaluation of teamwork in the performing arts. We conducted structured interviews with leaders of 12 performing arts, including dance, improv theater, jazz, orchestra, straight theater, and others. We found that the need for team training, other than just rehearsal, depended on the structure of the teams, particularly the role played by the team leader.

Another study compared improv comedy teams to NASCAR pit crews to Waffle House server teams. All of these teams have clear expectations of their team members relative to their respective tasks. There were commonalities that we had not expected. For example, all three teams were well aware that they were performing for their audiences.

AIDING

The predictor displays for air traffic controllers that I discussed in Chapter 2 are an example of directly augmenting human performance. I pursued a variety of studies of aiding at MIT, Illinois, and Georgia Tech, translating the findings of these studies into market offerings at Search Technology, Enterprise Support Systems, and, most recently, Curis Meditor.

I came to focus on a class of aiding termed decision support systems, with emphasis on supporting the decision making of operators, maintainers, and designers of complex systems such as aircraft and power plants. When I was a graduate student at MIT, the early days of artificial intelligence were flowering. It was natural for me to wonder how this technology could support operators and maintainers.

At that time, engineering psychologist Paul Fitts and human factors engineer Alphonse Chapanis were famous for MABA–MABA lists, which refer to "Men Are Better At, Machines Are Better At" lists of functions that should be assigned to humans or machines. By the way, it took until 1980 or so before the topic of man-machine systems was replaced by human–machine systems.

The intent of these lists was to support system designers to address the allocation of functions between humans and machines. It struck me that the answer to the question of who should do what might be: "It all depends." I came up with the idea of adaptively allocating functions or tasks depending on the circumstance. Before long, I simplified the notion to adaptive aiding.

I published my first paper on this topic in 1976. Our various studies of multi-task decision making and adaptive aiding were discussed in Chapter 2. A considerable body of research results and aiding concepts emerged that contributed to the intelligent aiding concept discussed in the next section.

Within a couple of years, I became very interested in human error. Procedures are a type of job aid. The idea is still to tell humans exactly what to do. If they vary from the procedure steps, it is an error. The problem is when they should vary because the assumptions upon which the procedures are based are not valid in the current circumstances. Then, we value humans' abilities to innovate.

Sometimes, however, these innovations are not the right actions. Then, we term them errors. It seemed to me that errors are side effects of flexibility. It also struck me that errors are not as much a problem as the consequences of errors. Perhaps we could monitor humans' actions and make sure they understood what they did and help them to avoid or minimize the consequences of these actions. The idea of error monitoring and error-tolerant human–system interfaces emerged. I discuss this in the next section.

Once I completed my PhD at MIT, I stayed on for one semester as a post-doc on Tom Sheridan's Community Dialog Project. The idea was to support citizens involved with social decision making. We used multi-stakeholder, multi-attribute utility theory to help groups define and rank alternatives, via computer displays and inputs through hand-held devices. This was before wireless capabilities, so the meeting rooms were laced with cables from each hand-held device to the computer.

We worked with groups at universities, government labs, and community groups. The group I remember best was a group of clergypersons from Protestant, Catholic, and Jewish congregations that met weekly in Harvard Square. They wanted to discuss and rank order approaches to creating a "fair" income tax. This required that we create a database of national income by levels and the number of people at each level.

The constraint was that any income tax scheme had to generate enough revenue to meet federal budget needs. They thought this would be easy. Someone suggested a 100% tax on incomes above $100,000 – keep in mind that this was 50 years ago. I remember reporting, "Ok, you have achieved 5% of the national budget. What next?" The group was crestfallen.

They, regretfully, had to tax the middle class. They discussed and evaluated various schemes, inching their way to the national budget. They found it very frustrating. Finally, one clergyman said, "This is too complex for me. Let's leave it to Congress. It's their job." I suggested that they had at least proven to themselves that almost all of their simple ideas would not work. They agreed.

In Chapter 3, I discussed our research on libraries and information networks. By the late 1970s, computer-based information retrieval systems were emerging, forerunners of Google by two decades. Researchers would type in queries, often with logical specifications such as AND, OR, or NOT. This would result in a list of titles and sources of references that matched the query. In some cases, there would be abstracts and reference lists as well.

The National Science Foundation funded our efforts to develop aiding for researchers doing this task. We created an experimental system, DBASE, and an associated large database of synthetic research articles on agriculture. Subjects in our studies were asked to answer questions such as "Does fertilizer X in climate Y substantially increase the yield for crop Z?"

Having designed the database, we knew that all the questions were answerable. In fact, there were often multiple synthetic articles that provided relevant evidence upon which to base answers. We were interested in the strategies that people employed to find the answers. It was by no means as simple as just typing in the question we had posed to them.

People were not very skilled at formulating their queries. Consequently, they retrieved many references of little use. They would eventually find a useful thread and immediately recognize highly relevant references. We developed an aiding scheme whereby their original query was automatically reformulated so that the article they valued greatly was the first hit. This dramatically improved their performance.

My interest in this topic has remained. For the last ten years or so, I have been working with David Seuss at Northern Light using his SinglePoint platform to host my current research portal *Curis Meditor*, which is Latin for health best practices. This portal has been central to studies of cancer control, the opioid epidemic, and assistive technologies for disabled and older adults.

The portal includes aggregated content for 40 million research articles and abstracts, as well as 50,000 English language articles – per day. To help one digest such a massive amount of information, Northern Light has created machine learning capabilities that "read" the articles for you and synthesize insights in the context of your query. When you find the high-value articles you are seeking, you click on More Like This, and it reformulates the query, as explained above, and re-executes the search.

Users of the *Curis Meditor* portal have offered comments like, "I just did several days' work in two hours." Another said, "This is a killer app." This is not automating research. It is augmenting human-centered research activities. Humans decide what is of interest and recognize it when it is found. As smart as *Curis Meditor* seems, it has no interests, and no research agenda of its own. I return to augmented intelligence later in this chapter.

INTELLIGENT AIDING

What aiding functions are needed to augment human intelligence? One function is information management. This involves information selection (what to present) and scheduling (when to present it). Information modality selection involves choosing among visual, auditory, and tactile channels. Information formatting concerns choosing the best levels of abstraction (concept) and aggregation (detail) for the tasks at hand. Aiding can be used to make all these choices in real time as the human is pursuing the tasks of interest.

Another function is intent inferencing. Information management can be more helpful if it knows both what humans are doing and what they intend to do. Norm Geddes found that representing humans' task structures in terms of goals, plans, and scripts can enable making such inferences. Scripts are sequences of actions which are connected to information and control requirements. When the aiding infers what you intend to do, it then knows what information you need and what controls you want to execute it.

One of the reasons that humans are often included in systems is that they can deal with ambiguity and figure out what to do. Occasionally, what they decide to do has potentially unfortunate consequences. In such cases, "human errors" are reported. Errors in themselves are not the problem. The consequences are the problem.

For this reason, another function is error monitoring. This requires capabilities to identify and classify errors, which are defined as actions that do not make sense (commissions) or the lack of actions (omissions) that seem warranted at the time. Identification and classification lead to remediation. This occurs at three levels: monitoring, feedback, and control. Monitoring involves the collection of more evidence to support the error assessment. Feedback involves making sure the humans realize what they just did. This usually results in humans immediately correcting their errors. Control involves automation taking over, e.g., applying the brakes, to avoid imminent consequences.

The notion of taking control raises the overall issue of whether humans or computers should perform particular tasks. There are many cases where the answer is situation dependent. Thus, this function is termed adaptive aiding. The overall concept is to have mechanisms that enable real-time determination of who should be in control. Such mechanisms have been researched extensively, resulting in a framework for design that includes principles of adaptation and principles of interaction. I proposed the First Law of Adaptive Aiding – *computers can take tasks, but they cannot give them*.

Another function is intelligent tutoring to both train humans and keep them sufficiently in the loop to enable successful human task performance when needed. Training usually addresses two questions: (1) how the system works and (2) how to work the system. Keeping humans in the loop addresses maintaining competence. Unless tasks can be automated to perfection, humans' competencies need to be maintained. Not surprisingly, this often results in training vs. aiding tradeoffs, which I later discuss.

Many of the earlier research and applications of the notions just elaborated focused on the operation and maintenance of complex engineered systems such as aircraft, power plants, and factories. The tasks associated with such systems are usually well understood. One application we addressed focused on electronic checklists for aircraft pilots. The results were sufficiently compelling to motivate the inclusion of some of the functionalities we evaluated on the Boeing 777 aircraft.

We developed a conceptual architecture for intelligent interfaces and applied it several times to tasks that are sufficiently structured to be able to make the inferences needed to support the functionality just outlined. The overall architecture for augmenting intelligence follows a particular logic:

- Humans see displays and controls and decide and act. Humans need not be concerned with aspects other than these three elements of the architecture. The overall system frames humans' roles and tasks and provides support accordingly.
- The intent inference function infers what task(s) humans intend to do. This function retrieves information and controls needs for these task(s). The information management function determines displays and controls appropriate for meeting information and control needs.
- The intelligent tutoring function infers humans' knowledge and skill deficits relative to these task(s). If humans cannot perform the task(s) acceptably, the information management function either provides just-in-time training or informs adaptive aiding (see below) of the humans' need for aiding.
- Deep learning neural nets provide recommended actions and decisions. The explanation management function provides explanations of these recommendations to the extent that explanations are requested.
- The adaptive aiding function, within the intelligent interface, determines the humans' role in execution. This can range from manual to automatic control, with execution typically involving somewhere between these extremes. The error monitoring function, within the intelligent interface, detects, classifies, and remediates anomalies.

Note that these functions influence each other. For example, if adaptive aiding determines that humans should perform task(s), intelligent tutoring assesses the availability of necessary knowledge and skills and determines training interventions needed, and information management provides the tutoring experiences to augment knowledge and skills. On the other hand, if adaptive aiding determines that automation should perform task(s), intelligent tutoring assesses humans' abilities to monitor automation, assuming such monitoring is needed.

The overall architecture includes explicit and implicit learning loops. The statistical learning loop continually refines the relationships in its layers, either by supervised learning or reinforcement learning. This will involve balancing exploration (of uncharted territory) and exploitation (of current knowledge). This is likely to involve human designers and experimenters. Of particular interest is how aiding will forget older data and examples that are no longer relevant, e.g., a health treatment that has more recently been shown to be ineffective.

Rule-based learning loops are concerned with inferring rule-based explanations of the recommendations resulting from statistical learning and inferring human decision makers' intentions and state of knowledge. Further, learning by decision makers is facilitated by the tutoring function.

Thus, the intelligent aiding will be learning about phenomena, cues, decisions, actions, etc., in the overall task environment. The decision makers will learn about what the aiding is learning, expressed in more readily understandable rule-based forms. The intelligent support system will be learning about the decision makers' intentions, information needs, etc., as well as influencing what the decision makers learn.

AUGMENTED INTELLIGENCE

The above concepts and principles were employed to design, develop, and evaluate intelligent decision support for fighter pilots and aircraft designers. The former project was called Pilot's Associate and was supported by Defense Advanced Research Projects Agency (DARPA). The latter was called Designer's Associate and was supported by the Air Force. These were the two largest projects in the history of Search Technology and caused us to grow to almost 40 employees.

These ambitious projects carefully integrated information management, intent inferencing, error tolerance, and adaptive aiding, leveraging our many studies of these concepts. We knew what worked and what did not. Nevertheless, integrating these concepts into the overall Pilot's Associate, in particular, was a substantial challenge. Several companies were contributing key elements of the overall set of capabilities. Making sure everything worked together required careful coordination.

These projects caused us to reflect on whether one should automate human intelligence or, instead, focus on augmenting human intelligence. The implications are fairly clear. To the extent that decisions emanating from artificial intelligence (AI)-based capabilities are always 100% correct, then the action systems, human or otherwise, can simply execute the recommended decisions.

If recommendations will occasionally be rejected, or should be rejected, then the typical minimal explanation capabilities of AI will impose responsibilities on humans that will require decision support. This suggests the need for an intelligent interface layer between the AI capabilities and the action systems, particularly when human decision makers are ultimately responsible for decision making. This amounts to aiding to use the aiding.

In the past few years, I have been focused on cognitive assistants for engineers, clinicians, and disabled and older adults. These AI-based assistants help with engineering problem solving, medical diagnoses and treatments, and transportation via driverless cars. We have developed use cases in terms of stories of these assistants interacting with humans in performing these tasks.

Once targeted users find these story-based use cases compelling, we then decompose the stories into functions, inputs, and outputs that are mapped to technologies. We then assess the maturity of these technologies to decide on the capabilities needed for the initial version of the cognitive assistant. Typically, this first version is rather simple compared with the full capabilities portrayed in the story. Nevertheless, the story remains the vision.

This process can be characterized as starting with the user experience (UX). Once that is satisfactory, we move on to the user interface (UI). Next comes technology capabilities and then actual design. This is sometimes termed the UX-UI approach to design. I have found that this leads to much more well-founded conceptual designs and, subsequently, significantly fewer ad hoc detailed designs. I return to this concept in Chapter 11.

TRAINING VS. AIDING TRADEOFFS

How do you decide whether to enhance people's potential to perform via training or directly augment people's performance via aiding? We studied this question for the Air Force and developed a tool with the unsurprising name TRAIDOFF. The overall purpose was to aid designers in choosing the balance between training and aiding.

Why is this tradeoff important? Upstream design decisions strongly impact downstream manpower, personnel, and training (MPT) requirements. However, these considerations are quite distant organizationally, and in time. MPT decisions are made after design decisions are frozen. Further, as one Navy executive told me, "At the level at which people actually understand this tradeoff, they have no authority to address it. At the level where people have the authority to address the tradeoff, they do not understand it."

We identified 29 approaches to addressing training versus aiding. There were three categories: general guidelines, performance predictions, and behavior predictions. The information sources utilized by these approaches included judgment, archives, and models. This led to the formulation of three analytic techniques: status quo, driven by historical data; performance, based in terms of how well people perform; and behavior, based in terms of information sought and actions taken.

TRAIDOFF was a software-based tool that supported a systematic 15-step process. Three prototypes were created. The first only supported one use case – training and aiding long-haul truck drivers. The second prototype differentiated the computer-based support for novices, journeymen, and experts. These three categories differ enormously in terms of what you can assume people know.

The third tradeoff involved a panel of experts, embodied in AI expert systems. This was prompted by the recognition that human training experts tend to advocate training while human aiding experts tended to advocate aiding. Representing these different perspectives resulted in a panel that provided conflicting advice. Nevertheless, TRAIDOFF was well received by training and aiding experts.

Thus, we know how to address training versus aiding tradeoffs. However, the aforementioned organizational barriers remain. I served on a DoD advisory committee on modeling and simulation. Senior military members of this advisory committee commented that simulations are not built until the system design is finalized. The two members of the committee with substantial commercial experience – the chief technology officer (CTO) of a game company and me – argued that you should simulate the system before you finalize its design. This enables getting users involved long before most design decisions are made.

Nevertheless, this organizational disconnect persists. It reflects the way DoD acquires systems. The government envisions missions and formulates the requirements for the capabilities to conduct that these missions must satisfy. These requirements form the basis for requests for proposals to which private industry responds. The winner of the competition builds the capabilities and delivers them. The government then works out the MPT requirements to successfully deploy the capabilities. They then may discover that resolving MPT issues will be difficult and very expensive.

There have been proposals for concepts such as concurrent engineering, where training and aiding are designed in parallel rather than in series. As reasonable as this sounds, the stewards of the status quo have successfully thwarted adoption. This is due in part to the public–private collaboration needed to succeed. The DoD's culture of arms-length relationships with contractors underlies these barriers.

CONCLUSIONS

This chapter has addressed enhancing people's potential to perform via training, or directly augmenting people's performance via aiding. Somewhat simplistically, the question is whether you put the smarts in the people or in the machines. Numerous pundits have argued that the pace of technology will inevitably result in machines doing an increasing portion of all jobs.

To an extent, this is likely to happen. However, other projections suggest that many millions of new jobs will be created for the skilled technical workforce. This workforce will need the knowledge and skills to operate and maintain our increasingly complex systems, ranging from energy and transportation to food and water. Everything will be laced with sensors and highly networked – and will occasionally fail.

The skilled technical workforce will need to be capable of detecting, diagnosing, and remediating failures. This workforce will need to be highly trained. They will also need aiding to support their successful performance of these tasks. The training and aiding will need to be integrated to provide, for example, just-in-time training in how to use some aspects of the aiding.

There is widespread agreement that the skilled technical workforce will need education beyond K–12. However, four-year college education will probably not be needed. Two-year programs at community colleges, coupled with employer-based training, are likely to fit the bill. My quick, but likely too simple, calculation is that we will need to triple the capacity of community colleges to provide the talent pipeline needed for these jobs.

EPILOGUE

We conducted a series of studies on human detection, diagnosis, and compensation for systems failures in a simulated environment named PLANT – Production Levels and Network Troubleshooting. We focused primarily on what operators need to know to perform well. We developed rule-based models of each operator using a framework called KARL – Knowledgeable Application of Rule-Based Logic.

The idea emerged to use the models of each operator as an assistant to each operator. In other words, each person's assistant was a computational model of himself or herself. Thus, the "second opinion" provided was very much biased to agree with the operator's own opinion. In general, this assistant improved detection, diagnosis, and compensation in terms of faster responses and fewer errors.

One of the failures of PLANT was a safety system failure. The safety system was designed to trip (shut off) pumps and valves when fluid levels became too high or low. The safety system failure resulted in random trips unrelated to fluid levels. Operators were told about this possibility, but their training did not include experiencing it.

None of the operators without the computational assistant were successful in dealing with this one-time failure. They were rather confused by it. Most of the operators with the assistant correctly diagnosed this failure and shut the safety system off. Their computational assistant had no knowledge of the possibility of a safety system failure. In fact, KARL's consistent advice was that nothing was wrong.

The operators reacted to this advice, saying something like, "No, everything is not fine. Something unusual has happened." They then correctly diagnosed the safety system failure.

The key point here is that bad advice improved performance. This suggests that there are subtleties to the impacts of intelligent assistance. Augmented intelligence can result even when the computer is a flawed assistant. This phenomenon merits much more research, but this result does emphasize the possibility of unexpected outcomes.

FURTHER READING

Rouse, W.B. (2007). *People and Organizations: Explorations of Human-Centered Design*. New York: Wiley.

Rouse, W.B. (2019). *Computing Possible Futures: Model Based Explorations of "What if?"* Oxford, UK: Oxford University Press.

Rouse, W.B. (2021). *Failure Management: Malfunctions of Technologies, Organizations, and Society*. Oxford, UK: Oxford University Press.

5

Human-Centered Design

PROLOGUE

Whose preferences should influence decisions regarding the design of products and services? In some situations, there may be one ultimate decision maker, although this is very rare beyond individual consumer decisions. Success usually depends on understanding all stakeholders. My approach to such understanding I termed human-centered design.

In contrast with the broadly articulated concept of user-centered design, human-centered design addresses the concerns, values, and perceptions of all stakeholders in designing, developing, deploying, and employing products and services. The basic idea is to delight primary stakeholders and gain the support of the secondary stakeholders. This objective can be pursued very systematically.

This notion first occurred to me at a workshop in the late 1980s at the NASA Langley Research Center near Hampton, Virginia. Many participants were discussing pilot-centered design that focused on enhancing aircraft pilots' abilities, overcoming pilots' limitations, and fostering pilots' acceptance. I suggested that we should do this for all the human stakeholders involved in the success of an aircraft program. People asked what I specifically meant.

I responded, "Pilots may fly them, but they don't build them or buy them!"

In other words, pilots being supportive of design choices may be necessary for success, but it is not sufficient. The airlines have to want to buy the airplanes, the aerospace companies have to be willing to produce them, and regulatory bodies have to certify the use of the planes. The buyers, builders, and regulators have criteria beyond those important to pilots.

DOI: 10.4324/9781003365549-5

INTRODUCTION

I have elaborated on the human-centered design construct and an associated methodology in short courses that I taught across the USA, and in Europe, Asia, and Africa. Students in these courses commented that my slides captured the methodology, but not the rich set of stories I wove through my expositions. This led to several books that I published in the 1990s. The human-centered design methodology has been applied many times and continually refined and elaborated in several more recent books.

The premise of human-centered design is that the major stakeholders need to perceive policies, products, and services to be valid, acceptable, and viable. Valid policies, products, and services demonstrably help solve the problems for which they are intended. Acceptable policies, products, and services solve problems in ways that stakeholders prefer. Viable policies, products, and services provide benefits that are worth the costs of use. Costs here include the efforts needed to learn and use policies, products, and services, not just the purchase price.

The overall approach presented in this chapter is intended to increase validity, acceptability, and viability. This is often challenging. First and foremost are viability challenges. Often, much time and money go into developing aspects of solutions that, at least in retrospect, were not needed to address the problems of primary interest. Consequently, stakeholders feel the benefits of solutions are not worth the costs.

Second are acceptability issues. Many key stakeholders are not educated in analytic methods and tools. Nevertheless, they are often highly talented, have considerable influence, and will not accept that the optimal policy, somehow magically produced, is X equals 12. We need methods and tools that are more engaging for these types of stakeholders.

Third are validity issues. There is often concern that overall analyses are of questionable validity. This concern is due in part to the possibility that assumptions are inconsistent across component analyses. There is also the issue of incompatible definitions of organizational states across component analyses, which can lead to misleading or incorrect results. This is particularly plaguing when one is unaware of these incompatibilities.

The overall human-centered approach overcomes these issues in several ways. The early steps of the methodology focus on problem formulation, with particular emphasis on interactive pruning of the problem space prior to any in-depth explorations. In-depth analyses tend to be expensive, so it is important to be sure they are warranted.

Second, we have found that key stakeholders value being immersed in interactive visualizations of the phenomena, and relationships among phenomena associated with their domain and the questions of interest. This enables them to manipulate controls and explore responses. This is typically done in a group setting with much discussion and debate.

Third, the overall approach explicitly addresses agreeing on a consistent set of assumptions across analyses. This need prompts delving into the underpinnings of each type of analysis. The overarching question is whether connecting multiple types of analysis will yield results that are valid in the context of the questions at hand.

All of these human-centered design concepts come together in Figure 5.1 using four frameworks. Set-based design is an approach, developed by Toyota, that involves formulating multiple design concepts, often investing in multiple alternatives rather than trying to choose only one

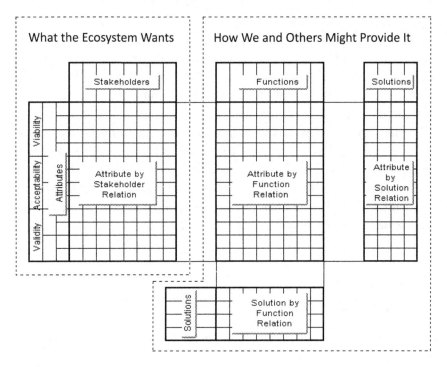

FIGURE 5.1
Human-Centered Design Framework.

for investments. From a human-centered perspective, this enables keeping stakeholders involved who may not prefer the highest ranked choice.

Quality function deployment represents the "voice of the stakeholders" in terms of what attributes matter most to each stakeholder or class of stakeholders, expressed in terms of utility functions that map physical scales to common utility scales. Design structure matrices enable representing the structure of solutions in terms of how elements of the systems affect each other. This is helpful when formulating tradeoffs.

Multi-attribute utility theory is used to roll up stakeholders' preferences for each of the alternative solutions. A multi-stakeholder model is used to aggregate preferences across stakeholders. One can vary the weights in the stakeholder models and in the aggregate model to assess the sensitivity of the ranking of alternatives to assumed weightings.

Thus, we can calculate the expected utilities of alternatives. One can then choose the alternative with the highest expected utility. My experience is that this seldom happens. While one or more alternatives may seem to predominate, decision makers want to understand how alternative assumptions affect this dominance.

For example, they may see that alternative X prevails with particular assumptions, while alternative Y may seem stronger with another set of assumptions. I have found that insightful decision makers will then turn to the group and ask, "What creative changes could we make so that these two outcomes are not so different?"

The analytic platform then becomes a means for exploring various "what if?" scenarios. What if company A invested in company B to develop a technology that will enable particular outcomes? But, isn't that risky? Perhaps, but we can address that later. Could that make the difference in the competition? The abilities to mutually and creatively explore "what if?" are often the key to new futures.

CASE STUDIES

The proof is in the pudding. In other words, the value of human-centered design can be ascertained by applying this approach to planning and developing new products and services. That's what we did. We worked with over 20 major companies and agencies in the USA, as well as Europe,

Asia, and Africa, to refine this approach and, as I explain in Chapter 6, develop a suite of software tools to support the application of human-centered design.

We worked with Air Force Research Laboratory, Boeing, Lockheed, and NASA to plan new aircraft, particularly new electronic aircraft cockpits. With Allied Signal, Honeywell, and Rolls Royce, we planned new aircraft engines and avionics systems. Our short course at NASA Langley Research Center led to suggestions that my forthcoming book on human-centered design be renamed *Design for Success*, to which the publisher happily agreed.

My first extensive engagements in the automobile industry began with Rover, planning for the Land Rover, MGB, and the early design of the Mini Cooper, before Rover was acquired by BMW. I then worked with Raytheon on automotive avionics. I worked with General Motors (GM) to understand what differentiated vehicles' successes from failures. Most recently, I have worked with GM on planning driverless cars for disabled and older adults.

I discussed my immersion in the world of cars in Chapter 1. These early experiences made my involvement with these companies more fascinating as they enabled me to see beyond the dealers' showrooms into the bigger picture of how new vehicles were conceptualized, designed, and manufactured.

Quite a few engagements involved computers and communications. We engaged with Digital Equipment Corporation, Harris, Motorola, and SEMATECH on semiconductors and with DRS Technologies, Microelectronics and Computer Consortium, and Motorola on electronics. We worked with Digital on microprocessors and Raytheon on optical computing.

We helped plan new communications satellites with Honeywell, Hughes, and the Singapore Ministry of Defense. Hitachi and Johnson Controls were clients for planning new industrial control systems. Numerous smaller companies in these industries were also clients. Overall, we worked with well over 100 companies and agencies via a few hundred engagements.

The engagements with these organizations over 10+ years enabled substantial refinement and extensions of our approach to human-centered design. In this process, several thousand executives, managers, and subject matter experts from engineering, manufacturing, marketing, finance, and other disciplines contributed to these refinements and extensions. The result was the body of knowledge and software tools discussed in Chapter 6.

As our product planning engagements steadily increased, we started to gain attention from corporate executives above the engineering and technology functions. A South African executive told us he was impressed with our approach to the human-centered design of their products and services. Could we help him with the overall enterprise? How could he create a human-centered enterprise?

This led to our approach to business planning, embodied in my next book, *Strategies for Innovation*, and a new workshop. A key element of our approach to business planning was the success hierarchy.

At the highest level, success potential is composed of two components: market potential and technology potential. Market potential, in turn, is composed of potential unit sales and potential revenue per unit. Technology potential is composed of technology importance and technology position.

These four attributes are further decomposed into eight attributes. Potential unit sales are determined by market size and market share. Potential revenue per unit is influenced by the benefits of the solution offered and the level of competition. Technology importance is determined by customer technology orientation and alternatives to your technology. Technology position is composed of technology know-how and domain know-how.

We used the success hierarchy to diagnose problems with plans and determine how they could most readily be improved. A few rules of thumb emerged from the repeated use of this tool:

- It is easier to change the characteristics of the enterprise than it is to change the characteristics of the market.
- It is easier to change to a different market segment than it is to change the characteristics of a market segment.
- It is easier to acquire domain know-how by hiring people with this know-how than it is to acquire technology know-how by creating it.

A few vignettes illustrate how the success hierarchy prompted important insights.

One vignette concerned a small manufacturer of medical monitoring equipment that was attempting to expand the market for its products. Evaluation of this company's plans using the hierarchy led to the conclusion that it needed to position its products in a way to lessen the number of competitors. This conclusion led to the realization by the CEO that, within the expanded market, they actually did not know whether there was little or some competition. Once he realized how critical this issue was, he decided to perform a much more extensive market assessment.

In another vignette, a small manufacturer of circuit boards for personal computers had developed a board to assure database security for banking applications. The use of the hierarchy resulted in the conclusion that the company was woefully deficient in domain expertise in banking. This caused the CEO of the company to consider more seriously a joint venture proposal that they had received from another company with extensive domain know-how in banking.

A Fortune 500 aerospace company was faced with strong market demand for a new subsystem to be added to the systems they were currently selling and intending to sell. Evaluation of their initial plan to meet this need identified that their greatest weakness was in the technology know-how necessary to design and develop this new subsystem. This conclusion supported their tentative decision to subcontract this effort.

An R&D function within a Fortune 500 computer company was concerned with its plan to provide technical services to operating divisions in the company. Evaluation of their plan led to the conclusion that their technology know-how, supposedly their primary value added, was only strong rather than very strong. Further, their domain know-how was modest. On the technology know-how side, their problem was a lack of bench strength – not enough qualified people to satisfy the projected demands. This analysis led to the conclusion that they should bolster their bench strength by adding people with the needed technology know-how and relevant domain experience.

Our methodologies for product and business planning were not always adequate. Sometimes, strategy discussions and debates reached impasses. The two (or more) sides to these debates fundamentally disagreed with each other. I became very interested in the underlying basis for these disagreements.

Consider a few examples. A planning team in a semiconductor company faced strongly conflicting beliefs about the extent to which the waste products from their operations were toxic. A team in an electronics company was entertaining broadening their offerings to include both defense and commercial products. The disagreement was about the extent you can sell high-tech products in commercial markets – rather quaint in retrospect.

An automobile company had announced tremendous quality improvement from its total quality management program. The disagreement emerged from the personnel in manufacturing who had never implemented the program, despite all the snazzy posters throughout the company's factories extolling the program.

These experiences led to our approach to organizational change, embodied in my next book, *Catalysts for Change*, and a new workshop. A key element of our approach was a model developed to address conflicts and disagreements.

Conflicting positions on strategies can be understood in terms of needs, beliefs, perceptions, and decisions. Perceived attributes of alternative courses of action influence people's decision making regarding whether or not they support a course of action. There is considerable debate about how decision making happens. Do people analytically weigh the attributes of alternatives? Or, do they react holistically to the pattern of attributes of each alternative?

We considered how perceptions are formed rather than how decisions are made. The motivation for this emphasis is quite simple. Focusing on people's perceptions of a course of action and assuring that these perceptions are positive, often by modifying the proposed course of action, can result in their supporting the course of action designed in this way.

The conventional model represents perceptions as being influenced by a person's knowledge and the information presented to them. Succinctly, people's knowledge gained via education and experience combines with the information available to them, the facts at hand, to yield perceptions.

Viewed very broadly, this model seems quite reasonable. However, the simplicity of this model can lead to inappropriate conclusions. If people's perceptions are other than desired, two courses of action are possible. One can modify the information available and/or educate them to modify and extend their knowledge. In doing so, your goal would be to "correct" misperceptions.

This perspective can lead one to feel that people do not support the proposed course because they do not understand. For example, if people really understood nuclear engineering, they would know that nuclear power is safe and they would want nuclear power plants. If people really understood climate change, they would know that the actions being proposed make sense.

Obviously, this perspective leads to many unsupported initiatives. To enable change decisions, a more elaborate model is needed. What influences perceptions beyond knowledge or "facts in the head," and information or "facts at hand"? A general answer is that people have a tendency to perceive what they want to perceive. In other words, their a priori perceptions strongly influence a posteriori perceptions. This tendency is supported by the inclinations to gain knowledge and seek information that support expectations and confirm hypotheses.

These phenomena and a variety of related phenomena can be characterized in terms of the effects of people's needs and beliefs on their perceptions. We formulated this characterization in terms of the Needs-Beliefs-Perceptions Model. In the context of this model, perceptions that one finds disagreeable are not necessarily incorrect. They are just different.

For instance, socialists and capitalists may perceive solutions differently because of differing beliefs about the nature of people and the role of government. As another example, scientists and people who are not technically oriented may have differing perceptions about the impact of technology because of different needs and beliefs concerning the predictability of natural phenomena, desirability of technical solutions, and likely implementations of technologies.

Consider the likely determinants of needs and beliefs – nature and nurture. Nature includes genetic influences on needs and perhaps beliefs. Physical needs, for example, are obviously affected by inherited characteristics and traits. Characteristics such as stature, tendencies for baldness and poor eyesight, and vulnerabilities to particular diseases appear to be hereditary. Inheritance of psychological and social traits is a topic of continuing debate.

Nurture concerns the effects of childhood, education, cultural influences, work experience, economic situation, and so on. Clearly, factors such as work experience and economic situation can have a substantial impact on needs. Similarly, education and cultural influences can greatly affect beliefs.

Nature and nurture are included in this model to provide means for affecting needs and beliefs. While nature usually is only affected at the snail's pace of evolution, nurture can be more quickly influenced by modifying situations and hence experiences which, thereby, change needs and eventually beliefs, perceptions, and decisions.

I have used this model to address the aforementioned variety of conflict situations, ranging from quality improvement in an automobile company, to disagreements about environmental issues in a semiconductor company, and to attempts to transform an electronics company facing a loss of its primary market. I found that surfacing the needs and beliefs underlying conflicting perceptions was the key to making progress on these issues.

The needs and beliefs underlying these conflicts were found to be:

- Manufacturing personnel needed to be confident in top management's communications but did not believe announcements of the success of a program never implemented.
- Semiconductor engineers needed to feel they were not hurting the environment and consequently did not believe the waste chemicals were toxic.
- Defense engineers needed to feel they were working on the leading edge of technology and consequently did not believe that commercial technologies were the leading edge.

Training and better communications were the interventions that ameliorated these conflicts.

We now had three books and associated tools (see Chapter 6). I wondered whether the central concepts and principles could not be boiled down to the material that everyone would understand. The result was *Best Laid Plans*. Product planning was explained in the context of designing and fabricating furniture, one of my hobbies. Business planning was elaborated in the context of planning and conducting hikes, another one of my hobbies.

Change was considered in the context of discovery, the process of exploring and gaining insights into other cultures. This was prompted by the experience of marketing and selling our products and services in over 20 countries. I was away from the USA for roughly 25% of my time, teaching, selling, and most importantly, learning about how other cultures address decision making and risk, all from the perspective of the economics and politics in their country.

As the Internet bubble was about to burst in 2000 – more on this later – I was putting the finishing touches on the manuscript for a book that integrated across the previous books, *Essential Challenges of Strategic Management*. My business ventures had also been a large, long-term research project. I concluded that all enterprises face seven essential challenges.

These seven essential challenges of strategic management were identified in my explorations with thousands of executives and senior managers. These seven challenges are, by no means, a somewhat arbitrary set of important business issues. Instead, these challenges are key pieces of the strategy puzzle which fit together in particular and important ways.

Growth is the overarching goal and challenge of strategic management. Growth is essential to the well-being of an enterprise. Lack of growth leads, at best, to flat revenues and profits, if any, via cost cutting and eliminating anything not closely linked to sticking to the knitting. This, in turn, tends to limit opportunities for professional and personal growth and, in general, can create a pretty deadly organizational atmosphere.

At worst, lack of growth can lead to slow – or not so slow – declining revenues and profits. Cost cutting tends to become endemic and often severe. A "death spiral" can result where lack of discretionary resources leads to under-investment in those opportunities needed to just keep heads above water, which leads to further decreases in discretionary resources.

As one seasoned CEO put it, "Everyone makes mistakes and everyone encounters things which you cannot control. Growth is more forgiving." Thus, an enterprise must strategically focus on growth to assure – or at least increase the probabilities – that the downside is only a lack of growth rather than decline. This challenge is often on the top of managers' critical issues lists.

Value provides the foundation for growth. The reason an enterprise exists is to provide value to its stakeholders. Many organizations tend to think that the products and services they deliver are synonymous with the value they provide. However, stakeholders usually want the benefits of having these products and services rather than the artifacts or person-hours per se. In other words, the products and services are usually means, not ends.

Another common misperception is that what stakeholders valued in the past will continue to be what they value in the future. However, products and services may cease to provide the same benefits as in the past. Or, these benefits may be widely and inexpensively available. Consequently, relationships with markets change despite enterprises' assumptions to the contrary.

The challenge of value concerns matching stakeholders' needs and desires to the enterprise's competencies in the process of identifying high-value offerings that will justify the investments needed to bring these offerings to market. Ideally, this involves understanding and committing to innovation – creation of change via something new – in the targeted markets.

Focus concerns the challenge of deciding the path whereby the enterprise will provide value and grow. Focus involves making decisions to do some things, and not do others. It involves deciding to add value in particular ways, and not others. Thus, focus involves saying "yes" to a few things and "no" to many.

I have often found that "yes" is much, much easier than "no." Consequently, organizations end up dividing scarce resources among far too many things. Too few resources allocated to too many things leads to false starts and inadequate results. Everyone who won a little in the beginning loses a lot in the end.

The key to avoiding this dilemma is to define and communicate clear decision processes so that all stakeholders know what matters and how decisions are made. This allows decision makers to say "no" in the context of a well-understood framework. People will still be disappointed, but they usually will not perceive the decisions as unjust.

Change. Given a goal (growth), a foundation (value), and a path (focus), the next challenges concern designing an organization to follow this path, provide this value, and achieve this goal. Rarely is the current organizational design the right one for succeeding with these challenges.

Of course, the old organization is in place and, typically, the only source of sales and profits in the near term. Thus, how do you creatively design and build the new organization you need while also running the organization you've got – all with some degree of consistency and sanity?

This question is further complicated by the fact that the nature of organizations appears to be rapidly changing. Reengineering, downsizing, and rightsizing have changed the terms of the employer–employee social contract. Technology increasingly enables very mobile people and relationships – temporally, geographically, and organizationally. Change may be unavoidable, but there should be some strategic advantage gained in the process.

Future. The ways in which you address the challenge of the future strongly affect the most appropriate approaches to the challenges thus far discussed. The future is uncertain and risky and tends to be a long way off. Consequently, it is usually very difficult to estimate the value of the future. This typically results in heavy discounting of the future.

However, almost all the managers I have discussed this issue with readily agree that you have no choice but to invest in the future. You need a view of where you are headed and an investment portfolio aligned with this view. The question then becomes one of how to make these investment decisions. If we could buy an option in the future, how would we determine what this option is worth?

There are rigorous ways of addressing this question. Some of them borrow from sophisticated financial analysis methods. Others focus on decision-making processes and the multi-stage execution that should follow decisions. Making the case for the future is certainly a challenge, but this challenge is tractable.

Knowledge. The challenge of knowledge involves at the outset disentangling the term from marketing and sales pitches of all the vendors who stand ready to help you manage knowledge. Prior to managing knowledge, you need to how knowledge influences – or could influence – your enterprise's abilities to provide the value that is your foundation for growth.

More specifically, this challenge concerns understanding how to transform information into value-driven insights to strategic programs of action. This understanding should be gained in the context of critical business issues such as solution pricing or inventory control. In contrast, knowledge in general is seldom of much value – some would argue that it is not even knowledge.

Starting with critical business issues, one can determine what knowledge would make a difference and in what ways. This understanding should determine what information is relevant, how it is processed, and how its use is supported. While far from a panacea, this form of knowledge management can provide a substantial means to competitive advantage.

Time. Lack of time is almost always executives' and senior managers' most significant personal issue. People say that they spend too much time responding to often meaningless fire drills imposed by superiors, meeting with subordinates to make decisions that the subordinates should have made on their own, meeting in general, and responding to an increasingly overwhelming number of emails. The result, they report, is little time for addressing strategic challenges.

How managers invest their own time reflects their priorities and values, which are, of course, strongly affected by the social and cultural characteristics of an enterprise, and the business environment in general. The allocation of time also reflects the leadership style and abilities of managers. Inappropriate allocations of time and ineffective leadership go hand in hand.

Addressing the challenge of time involves first considering the roles of leaders in strategic management, and then the implications of these roles for how leaders allocate their time. What managers often fail to realize is that their time is one of their organization's scarcest resources. While money, at least in principle, is potentially unlimited, time is not.

In summary, there are relationships among challenges. Growth is the goal, and value provides the foundation for achieving this goal. Value influences choice of focus (path), investments in the future (view), and allocations of time (self). Focus affects time, and they both, in combination with the future, influence change (design). Future also affects knowledge that provides the means for addressing value. The view (future), path (focus), and design (change) combine to affect the goal (growth).

Clearly, the essential challenges of strategic management are highly interrelated. Dealing effectively with one or two challenges will not compensate for addressing the others poorly. Typically, the challenges presenting the greatest difficulties at the moment receive the most attention. This is understandable and appropriate, as long as managers keep all the challenges in perspective. Balancing how you address the whole set of challenges tends to be a challenge in itself.

It is useful to note that I have repeatedly tried to identify additional challenges or perhaps replace some of the above challenges with other, more compelling, or important challenges. I have been aided in this quest by managers at a wide variety of organizations where I have presented this overarching framework.

While there have been many suggestions, in-depth discussions of these alternatives have always resulted in retaining the set of challenges just elaborated without modifications. This does not mean, of course, that eternal truth has been found. Instead, it simply means that a large number of experienced, intelligent, and interested managers have found that this set of challenges works for them.

I returned to Georgia Tech in 2001 as chair of the top-ranked School of Industrial and Systems Engineering. I was convinced that this discipline should embrace complex enterprises, not in terms of the functional siloes that embody business schools. Civil engineers had roads and bridges, electrical engineering had electronics and computer hardware, mechanical engineering had automobiles and other vehicles, and computer science had algorithms and software. Industrial and systems engineering could have the enterprise. I return to this perspective in Chapter 7.

CONCLUSIONS

What is the biggest overarching challenge one has to face in planning new products and services, planning the enterprise's strategy, and addressing organizational change? Many executives and managers have expressed this succinctly – managing the company you have while creating the company you want. You have to, in effect, rewire the house with the power on.

There are often many possible ways to succeed. The tools discussed in Chapter 6 often provide the means for getting rid of bad ideas quickly. This enables focusing on and refining the good ideas that remain. These tools also enable the teams involved to see clearly the lines of reasoning, as well as supporting data, that justify the decisions leading the teams forward.

The human-centered design approach helps everyone on the team to understand all the stakeholders in terms of their values, concerns, and perceptions. This enables creating shared team mental models across functions and disciplines. I recall a planning workshop at a semiconductor company. A young electrical engineer approached me after the workshop to thank me. He then said, "I now know the variables of most importance to marketing, manufacturing, and finance. Before the workshop, I didn't even know the meanings of those variables."

EPILOGUE

The human-centered design construct has faced two impediments. First, the user-centered design community wants to equate humans with users. This community includes human factors, human–computer interactions, and psychology researchers and practitioners. My broadening of "human" to include marketing, manufacturing, finance, etc., requires understanding people beyond users and their tasks. This breadth is not compatible with the disciplinary orientation of this community. Consequently, these types of professionals were seldom my clients.

Clients tended to include vice presidents of R&D, engineering, and finance. They found my broader view reasonable and appealing. They were, however, often impatient. I addressed this in two ways. First, our workshops always focused on a market opportunity of great interest to them. At the end of the workshop, they had accomplished real work and made significant progress on something of importance to them.

Second, these engagements required only a few days. I started with five-day workshops but soon found that I could not keep important stakeholders engaged that long. We quickly evolved to two-day workshops. I explicitly asked important stakeholders to commit to these two days. I also performed significant pre-work so that the planning team could hit the ground running. The software tools discussed in Chapter 6 were also key to working quickly. We conducted hundreds of these workshops.

FURTHER READING

Rouse, W.B. (1991). *Design for Success: A Human-Centered Approach to Designing Successful Products and Systems.* New York: Wiley.

Rouse, W.B. (1992). *Strategies for Innovation: Creating Successful Products, Systems, and Organizations.* New York: Wiley.

Rouse, W.B. (1993). *Catalysts for Change: Concepts and Principles for Enabling Innovation.* New York: Wiley.

Rouse, W.B. (1994). *Best Laid Plans.* New York: Prentice-Hall.

Rouse, W.B. (2001). *Essential Challenges of Strategic Management.* New York: Wiley.

Rouse, W.B. (2007). *People and Organizations: Explorations of Human-Centered Design.* New York: Wiley.

6

Advisor Series of Software Tools

PROLOGUE

Microsoft was founded in 1975. VisiCalc, the first spreadsheet app, was introduced in 1979. The IBM PC was introduced in 1981, featuring Microsoft's DOS. Microsoft Windows arrived in 1985, followed by Microsoft Office in 1988.

Apple was founded in 1976. They introduced Apple II in 1977, Apple Mac in 1984, iPod in 2001, iPhone in 2007, and iPad in 2010. In the process, they transformed from a computer company into a digital device company.

The PC and the Mac quickly displaced Sun workstations, originally introduced in 1982, and Symbolics lisp machines in 1986. Our software engineering staff disdained the PC and Mac. They only wanted to work on leading-edge platforms. Symbolics disappeared in 1996, while Sun held on until 2010. PCs and Macs are now pervasive for all applications.

The ARPA Net was launched in 1969. The Internet was introduced in 1983. AOL arrived in 1985. Netscape was introduced in 1994, followed by Microsoft Explorer in 1995. Online search, retail, and social media followed, with Amazon in 1994, Google in 1998, Facebook in 2004, and Twitter in 2006.

This bit of history sets the stage for our pursuits in the software products' market. We wanted to create and sell shrink-wrapped software apps for business planning, product design, and market development. We proceeded to develop a suite of four tools. One was very successful, another moderately successful, and two others complemented the suite but generated quite modest revenues and profits.

DOI: 10.4324/9781003365549-6

INTRODUCTION

Our clients often asked about the design methodology that we employed to help them determine what their markets wanted and how they could meet these needs better than their competitors. They wanted a systematic model-based approach to making these determinations. As elaborated in Chapter 5, we proposed human-centered design, both philosophically and methodologically.

Boeing, Digital Equipment, Honeywell, Hughes, Lockheed, Motorola, Raytheon, and 3M were soon customers. Not long after, Hitachi, Rolls Royce, Rover, and other international organizations became customers. Our customer base became roughly 20 large technology-oriented companies and agencies.

We grew the company more by expanding across divisions of these enterprises than by recruiting totally new customers. As I recall, about 80% of our sales each year came from this customer base. These clients urged me to write the books I noted in Chapter 5. A few commented, "You're a college professor. This should be easy for you."

Once the books were provided during the workshops, participants had another suggestion. One participant put it crisply, "We don't really want to read these books. We would like tools such that in using the tools we would be inherently following the principles in the books." Another participant said, "We don't just want knowledge; we want executable knowledge."

We agreed with the idea, but we were very slow getting started. Finally, two customers, independently, offered to buy corporate-wide licenses for the tools even though they – and we – did not know what they were buying. The initial payments towards these licenses provided the resources to get started.

PRODUCT PLANNING ADVISOR

The first tool was the *Product Planning Advisor* (PPA). This tool embodied the principles of human-centered design discussed in Chapter 5. This eventually became our best-selling tool, but it did not get there smoothly. We followed our human-centered design methods much too literally.

We formed user groups at the two companies that had committed resources and asked everyone in both groups what they wanted the tool to do. We used this list of desires to build a tool that provided functions and features that *anybody* had requested. When we demonstrated the prototype, virtually every user was overwhelmed. We had provided what they wanted, but it had too many options, modes, etc.

We went back to the drawing board and redesigned PPA to only provide the functions and features that *everybody* had requested. This version was a success and we eventually sold many hundreds of copies to over 20 well-known companies. PPA was sold in conjunction with training workshops where participants learned human-centered design and the use of PPA, all in the context of real product planning problems of importance to their companies.

PPA is used to create and manipulate market and product models to explore the overall utility of both your current and anticipated offerings to the marketplace, as well as your competitors' offerings – as is depicted in Figure 5.1 in the previous chapter. The "What the Market Wants" element of the model characterizes the stakeholders in the product or service and their utility functions associated with context-specific attributes clustered in terms of validity, acceptability, and viability.

We assumed a common set of attributes across all stakeholders but, obviously, not everyone cares about everything, so for each stakeholder, many of the weights were zero. For example, the stakeholders might be the buyer of a product, the users of a product, and the maintainers of a product. The buyer will, of course, be concerned with the price of the product. The other two stakeholders may not be concerned with price.

Another element of the model underlying PPA concerns "How We and Others Will Provide It." This element specifies the attribute values associated with each solution. The functions associated with each solution are defined as well. Functions are things like steering, accelerating, and braking, as well as functions that may not be available in all solutions, e.g., a backup camera.

Attribute-to-function relationships were expressed on a scale with both positive and negative numbers. Positive numbers indicate that improving a function increases the attribute. Negative numbers indicate that improving a function decreases an attribute. For example, a backup camera may increase the price of the vehicle but decrease insurance costs. I elaborate on the use of these relationships below.

USING THE PRODUCT PLANNING ADVISOR

Once the PPA model is created, the planning team can use PPA to manipulate the model in several ways. Weightings can be varied – on a dashboard that displays them all in one place – to assess the sensitivity of utility rankings to such changes. Typically, people are concerned with how the rank ordering of solutions, ranked by utility, changes with such variations. In particular, what combinations of weightings lead to competitors' offerings having higher utilities?

One solution is often a strong competitor, namely, the status quo. In other words, customers may not buy anything. The status quo is compelling because the customer already has it and knows how to use it, and it requires little if any additional expenditures. I have found it quite interesting to see planning teams' reactions when they learn that their solution is worse than having nothing.

When teams encounter this situation or, more often, find the competitors' solutions to be superior to theirs, they will use PPA's "How to Improve" function to explore variations of the attributes and functions of their solutions. They can manipulate individual attributes or clusters of attributes to project the impacts of improvements of 10%, 20%, etc.

The hundreds of engagements with clients using PPA always involved multi-disciplinary teams, typically from marketing, engineering, manufacturing, finance, sales, and customer support. As noted in Chapter 5, clients often reported that planning sessions using PPA improved their team's mental models. They now knew what mattered to each functional area and how these concerns traded off across the preference space embodied in PPA.

Much to our surprise, the services associated with PPA and our other tools went well beyond training. We were repeatedly asked to facilitate workshops associated with new product planning endeavors, despite most of the participants in the workshops having been trained earlier. I asked a senior executive why these services were continually needed.

His response was, "I am not at all concerned with the costs of your software and services. I am totally concerned with the overall costs of success. Your involvement lowers those costs." Having facilitated hundreds of product planning workshops across many industries, we could share countless lessons learned. These cross-industry perspectives were highly valued.

APPLICATIONS

We conducted a very large number of new product planning engagements with a wide range of enterprises. In this section, I highlight six of these experiences.

As mentioned earlier, we worked with Rover on the initial conceptual design of the Mini Cooper, before Rover was bought by BMW, who then brought the Mini Cooper to market. We considered four stakeholders: young women, young men, young couples, and young couples with children. The design differences for each stakeholder were interesting. For example, the back seat plays a different role for couples with children. Young women and men differ in dashboard preferences.

An engagement with the government of Singapore focused on the viability of a very large unmanned aircraft to perform reconnaissance and surveillance over this island country. The public was a major stakeholder, but it was difficult to specify what the public wanted. A key insight was that the public wanted this airborne platform to succeed in the missions for which it was commissioned. Hence, these three missions were included as stakeholders in the PPA model.

While working with an aircraft engine company, we discovered that engineering and marketing disagreed about the units of measure of customers' key variables. This emerged because the PPA asks users to provide units of measure for all attributes. This was surprising because the leaders of these two functions had worked together for many years. They commented that they never had any reason in the past to discuss units of measure.

A semiconductor company was listed in the *Guinness Book of Records* for the speed of their microprocessors. Every product planning engagement with them included the objective that they retain their place in the record book. This was held of highest importance even for applications where the increased speed of the microprocessor provided no benefits to customers, due to limitations of the other elements of the system. They later relented on this objective.

We worked with an Israeli chemical company planning new pesticides and herbicides. They were required to test these products on rats to assure that they were not carcinogenic. They reported that none of the rats had gotten cancer because all of them died immediately upon ingesting the chemicals. However, this was inconsistent with the required testing protocol. This is one of the most unusual product planning engagements I ever experienced.

As noted earlier, Rolls Royce, a British aerospace company, acquired our product planning methods and tools. They were concerned about product support. We guaranteed them that any problem encountered or question that emerged would be solved or answered within 24 hours. We met this commitment, and the Managing Director, at a public industry meeting, commented that this quality of service was amazing and that he never before had experienced such responsiveness. The Internet and email enabled all of this.

BUSINESS PLANNING ADVISOR

As discussed briefly in Chapter 5, several of our clients asked us to assess their business processes. They liked our product planning process and wondered if we could help them by creating a similar tool for business planning. The *Business Planning Advisor* (BPA) was the result. It included a rule-based expert system that would assess a business plan in terms of the eight attributes of the success hierarchy discussed in Chapter 5 and then project the likelihood of success.

This tool faced a very competitive market where there were many business planning tools. Beyond the expert system embedded in BPA, our tool was not that different from the others. BPA was technically sound but did not yield the reactions – or sales – experienced with PPA. However, we needed to have a business planning offering as our customers expected it.

Nevertheless, we sold many business planning engagements. These experiences led us to realize that many clients did not really understand their market situations. Fairly often, we encountered perceptions that may have reflected past glories but did not capture current opportunities and threats. We also identified 13 delusions that often undermine strategic thinking.

SITUATION ASSESSMENT ADVISOR

This led us to the next book *Start Where You Are* and the *Situation Assessment Advisor* (SAA). This rule-based expert system assessed market situations based on users' answers to a large set of rather specific questions. SAA would assess the likelihood that an enterprise was in or headed to one or more of ten classic market situations.

An executive team at their annual planning offsite typically used SAA. It was well received. However, a company would buy one copy to use once per year. In contrast, they would buy 20–40 copies of PPA and use them frequently. SAA was a technical success but a market failure. We learned to focus on supporting tasks that are performed frequently by many people.

A companion tool to SAA was an expert system based on my next book, *Don't Jump to Solutions*. The purpose of this tool was to help users assess the extent to which they suffered from delusions in their perceptions of their company, markets, and technologies. We avoided the one-copy dilemma by selling this tool with the book which became the Main Selection of the Doubleday Executive Program Book Club. This book was recognized as one of the Top 20 global management books sold that year.

This tool was well received, but executives really liked the book, laced with stories about things that went wrong. The revenue from speaking opportunities and consulting engagements far surpassed the revenues from the book/tool product. It was becoming increasingly clear that the services associated with our tools were a major part of our business.

TECHNOLOGY INVESTMENT ADVISOR

The *Technology Investment Advisor* (TIA) provides a means of answering the question of what technology investments are worth, rather than what they cost. It is based on option pricing theory, which originated in the early 1970s for pricing financial options, e.g., the right but not a requirement to buy a company's shares at a future date at a price set now. Real options provide the right to pursue tangible outcomes such as technologies, processes, and capacities.

What is different about this? Traditional financial assessments focus on the net present value (NPV) of investments. Future cash flows are discounted by the interest rate that one needs to pay while waiting for these cash flows. This assumes that the investment is sustained even if the expected outcomes do not happen. Real options assume that investments are made for an initial period and only sustained if the options are "in the money"; that is, the value of exercising the options far exceeds the costs of exercising them.

Our initial exploration into using a real option approach to the valuation of technology investments was for the US Air Force. We quickly ran into difficulties, as the requisite data were unavailable. Motorola, another client at the time, soon invested in sustaining this exploration.

They posed the question as follows. They were then investing about 12% of revenues in R&D. This was based in part on the behaviors of their competitors, but they admitted that they had no idea whether this percentage should be higher or lower. In a two-day-long discussion of how to approach this issue, I suggested that we first discuss why it is not zero.

The response was straightforward. With zero investment, their business units would not have technological capabilities that provide competitive advantages. What advantages did they need? Performance, cost, and time to market were among their answers. I suggested that we think about how to provide technology options for these capabilities. This was serendipitous as Motorola's chief technology officer (CTO) had recently become interested in real options. We were off and running.

TIA emerged to function as follows. Production S-curves are used to project units sold over time, which plateau and then decline when new generations of products are introduced and begin to ascend their own S-curves. Production costs follow classical learning curves; e.g., every doubling of the number of units produced results in unit production costs of 60%–80% of the earlier costs. Making it down the learning curve, while maintaining prices, is key to steadily increasing profits unless all the competitors in the market are experiencing the same learning curves.

Projections of units produced, costs per unit, and prices per unit enable predictions of an enterprise's future financial statements based on the upstream options in which they have invested. The concern is with the option values of these possible futures. Typically, the option value (OV) has to be substantially higher than the option purchase price (OPP), i.e., net option value (NOV) has to be several multiples of OPP, for investment commitments to be made.

TIA was a proprietary software package with a dashboard allowing manipulations of various parameters, probability distributions of these parameters, and hence projected probability distributions of NOV, and numerous visualizations of projections. A few years ago, clients asked for an updated version of TIA. We found that the capabilities of Microsoft Excel had advanced sufficiently that the latest version of TIA could be fully accommodated in Excel. That is the version we have employed for our latest engagements.

TIA was often used in conjunction with PPA, which was used to determine the desired functions and features of a product of service, as well as the relative competitive advantages of alternative offerings. TIA is then used to project the financial attributes of the technologies needed to enable these offerings.

TYPICAL APPLICATIONS

Over the past 20 years, I have led roughly 30 engagements with clients interested in applying the real options approach to assessing the worth of technology investments. Roughly half of the engagements involved Lockheed Martin, 3M, Motorola, Raytheon, and the Singapore Ministry of Defense. The other engagements addressed consumer products, forest products, pharmaceuticals, publishing, and shipbuilding industries.

These engagements involved one or more of the following objectives:

- Investing in R&D. In many cases, options are bought by investing in R&D to create "technology options" that may, or may not, be executed in the future by business units.
- Running the Business. These examples are situations where the option was bought by continuing to operate an existing line of business, perhaps with modest current profitability but substantial future opportunities.
- Acquiring Capacity. These examples involve the possibility of acquiring the capacity to support market growth that is uncertain in terms of timing, magnitude, and potential profitability.

- Acquiring Competitor. These examples involve the possibility of acquiring competitors to support growth in current and adjacent markets that is uncertain in terms of timing, magnitude, and potential profitability.

For all four types of objectives, the option purchase involved an investment that was modest compared to the level of investment needed to exercise the option at a later date – if that made sense at that time. If the lion's share of the investment must be made upfront, then standard Net Present Value analyses are warranted rather than Net Option Value analyses.

ORGANIZATIONAL IMPLICATIONS

How does options-based thinking change the way an organization operates? Investment decision criteria change, as elaborated below. Beyond this direct change, there are broader organizational implications of adopting options-based thinking that I outline later in this section.

An enterprise simulation, *R&D World*, was used to assess the merits of alternative decision criteria for R&D investments. In this case study, Doug Bodner and I focused on R&D investments by a large forest products company. This simulation was used to compare criteria of NPV, NOV, and this company's other stage-gate criteria, e.g., competitive advantage and strategic fit.

The *R&D World* simulation was unveiled at a meeting of CTOs of leading forest products companies. Only one of the CTOs knew that the company being simulated was his. Each CTO was asked to propose what he or she would use for decision criteria. The 15 proposals were simulated for ten replications of 25-year periods. The resulting average profits ranged from a loss of $250 million to profits of $1.55 billion.

The CTOs were shocked. One commented, "I had no idea these criteria could make so much difference." A key distinction emerged. Emphasis on NPV preserves the R&D budget. Indeed, often the R&D budget was not fully expended due to a lack of positive NPV proposals.

In contrast, emphasis on NOV results in all, or nearly all, of the budget being expended. More projects are funded – modestly at first, as they are options. The company has more options that may (or may not) be exercised.

Rather than preserving the R&D budget, emphasis on NOV maximizes earnings per share. It seems reasonable to assume that this is the primary purpose of the R&D budget.

A good example is a small company selling wireless LAN technology. The chief financial officer (CFO) of the client company was considering shedding this provider of networking services to commercial customers. The business plan showed an NPV of $3 million, pretty small potatoes for a $20 billion parent company. We assessed the possibility of this company addressing the home networking market, which had not yet emerged.

The option was to simply keep running this small company while creating plans and capabilities to enter the home networking market. The NOV for this plan was $191 million. I was scheduled to present the results to the CFO. At the last minute, the VP with whom I had been working told me that my presentation could be only one slide. "Pick your best one," he said.

I entered the CFO's office and laid one page, a bar graph, on his conference table. One bar was $3 million high and labeled NPV. The other bar was $191 million high and labeled NOV. In typical CFO fashion, he asked, "What do I have to do to get the big bar?" I told him that he just had to keep the small company running until it was clear the home market was emerging, probably for about three years. Then, if warranted, he could exercise his option for $12 million. That is what he did.

Options-based thinking provides a framework for creating value-centered organizations. The first concern is *characterizing value*. Value is created in R&D organizations by providing "technology options" for meeting the contingent needs of the enterprise. In this way, R&D organizations provide a primary means for enterprises to manage uncertainty by generating options for addressing contingent needs. A central challenge for R&D organizations is to create a portfolio of viable options. Whether or not options are exercised is an enterprise challenge.

The next concern is *assessing value*. Value streams, or value networks, provide a means for representing value flow and assessing the value of options created. Valuation of R&D investments can be addressed by assessing the value of the options created in the value network. The options-based approach provides the means for this assessment.

A third and crucial concern is *managing value*. Decision-making processes – governance – are central to managing the flow of value. Specifically, if NOV is communicated as a key metric, then this metric should affect decisions. If other factors dominate, e.g., who knows whom, then emphases on NOV will be quickly and cynically dismissed.

The organizational structure affects value flow, with significant differences between hierarchical vs. heterarchical structures. In two studies of R&D organizations, one in industry and the other in government, we found that projects where appeal to the hierarchy for permission or resources was necessary resulted in delays of execution for months and sometimes years.

Individual and team affiliations and identities affect value flow; dovetailing processes with disciplines is essential. People need to be affiliated with value streams *and* their disciplinary base. Without the former, recognitions of contributions are likely diminished. Without the latter, disciplinary expertise can whither.

Champions play important, yet subtle, roles in value flow. Supporting champions is necessary but not sufficient for success. In one study, we encountered a situation where the deployment of R&D outcomes only occurred when champions found ways to circumvent processes intended to help them. This is not a sustainable approach to value.

Incentives and rewards affect value flow. Aligning these systems with value maximization is critical. If the incentive and reward systems remain aligned to outdated value propositions, people in the organization will continue to march to the old drummer. A good example is academia where multi-disciplinary research is extolled but incentives and rewards remain tightly tied to individual accomplishments.

Successful technology adoption depends on good ideas, adequate resources, and hard work, but that is not enough. Value needs to be characterized and assessed appropriately. Value needs to be managed to align behavioral and social phenomena with the value proposition being pursued. Misalignment can undermine ideas, resources, and outcomes.

ADVISOR SERIES

We marketed PPA, BPA, SAA, and TIA as the *Advisor Series* of planning tools. The relationships among these tools are shown in Figure 6.1. The basic idea was that companies would use SAA to assess their market situation, which would inform using BPA to formulate their business strategy, which would drive their use of PPA to plan product and service offerings, which

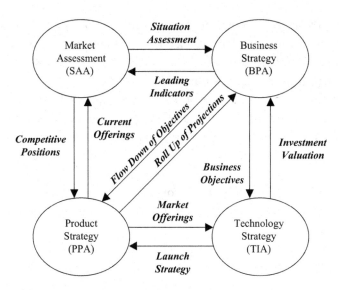

FIGURE 6.1
Advisor Series of Software Tools.

would be informed by the technology investment portfolio formulated with TIA to enable these offerings.

This provided a pretty compelling marketing story, but PPA and TIA dominated our engagements with clients. This was due, at least in part, to these tools being more sophisticated in terms of explicit models rather than more opaque expert systems. In other words, users created models with PPA and TIA that they could then use to explore various scenarios. With SAA and BPA, the underlying models were "hard wired."

We envisioned the flows between the four tools as being automatic, which would have been difficult to accomplish seamlessly. Fortunately, we never attempted this because customers had a better idea. They were all quite facile with Microsoft Excel. They would capture model outputs in Excel and then paste them into another model, with perhaps a bit of translation.

The reason they preferred this is that the Excel spreadsheet then became the "minutes" of the working session. Their confidence and expertise with Excel seemed to provide our tools more credibility. The ability to use their preferred representation, i.e., a spreadsheet, increased their level of comfort with the whole process. This is an important aspect of acceptability, as defined earlier.

Customers provided another important insight. The last step of the PPA process was Generate Documentation. Use of this step would automatically create a set of slides for use with Microsoft PowerPoint. This slide set would capture whatever elements of the product plan the users chose, via a dashboard designed for this. While customers asked for this function within PPA, they seldom used it.

A marketing executive at one of our clients explained this lack of use. He said that he used this function and brought the slide deck to a meeting with his boss for the purpose of requesting a budget to proceed. His boss asked how he had created the slides and the marketing executive opened his laptop and showed him PPA. His boss became intrigued, played around with various assumptions, considered alternative scenarios, and approved his budget. From then on, he always presented the tool itself, never the slides.

We have experienced this phenomenon repeatedly. When participants in PPA or TIA sessions can take the controls and explore possible futures, their buy in soars. They also become a rich source of ideas for improving models and visualizations. I think they were also tired of looking at PowerPoint slides.

EVALUATION

We conducted a study involving 100 planning teams and over 2,000 participants using one or more of the tools from the *Advisor Series*. Workshop participants were asked what they sought from computer-based tools for planning and design. Here is a summary of their responses:

- We want a clear and straightforward process to guide our decisions and discussions, with a clear mandate to depart from this process whenever we choose.
- We want the capture of information compiled, decisions made, and linkages between these inputs and outputs so that we can communicate and justify our decisions, as well as reconstruct decision processes.
- We want computer-aided facilitation of group processes via management of the nominal decision-making process using computer-based tools and large screen displays.

- We want tools that digest the information that we input, see patterns or trends, and then provide advice or guidance that the group perceives we would not have thought of without the tools.

Models and simulations can provide the "engine" that drives these capabilities, but greater advisory capabilities are needed to fully satisfy all these objectives. A good example comes from the networked version of PPA that enabled teams to work remotely and asynchronously. When asked what they liked best about this version, users did not comment on the modeling capabilities. Instead, they expressed great appreciation for a feature that was unique to this version.

The networked PPA kept "minutes" of every user transaction with the tool, including every proposed change and implemented change. Given that the tool knew each user and their issues of interest, we created a function called What's Happened Since I Was Last Here? When users clicked on this option, they were provided with an explanation of how their issues of interest were addressed while they were away. They found this invaluable.

The obvious conclusion from these lessons learned is that people want an environment that helps them address and solve their problems of interest. Computational models coupled with interactive visualizations provide some of this support. However, facilitation – human or otherwise – and capturing of "minutes" are also crucial elements of this support. They really like it when the support system surprises them with suggestions that, upon careful examination, are really good ideas.

The *Situation Assessment Advisor* and the assessment tool provided with *Don't Jump to Solutions* were rule-based expert systems. The rules for assessing market situations or organizational delusions were gleaned from extensive reviews of the literature, augmented with knowledge from our work with over 100 companies. I find it difficult to imagine how we would now do this with machine learning, as there are not thousands of documented examples of the 100 combinations of current and future market situations, nor of the many variations of 13 organizational delusions.

For both tools, management teams would answer a lengthy set of questions. For assessing their situation, the questions were about their markets, their positions in these markets, and their current and projected financial performance. For assessing organizational delusions, the questions related to their beliefs about their customers, offerings, organization, and competitors. Given their answers to these questions, the expert systems in the respective tools would display an assessment for the management team to discuss.

One of the best-liked features of these tools was their ability to present examples of what other companies with these assessments did and the extent to which these efforts succeeded or failed. Having ten or so examples of how other companies pursued change prompted much creative discussion by the teams. In fact, the assessments were, to an extent, just abstractions that enabled retrieving the kinds of examples that would motivate teams. One of the most important roles of our tools has been to enable and focus on the creativity of management teams.

CONCLUSIONS

I discuss many types of models in the various chapters of this book. However, none of these other models have been subject to as much evaluation as the *Advisor Series*. My experiences with these four tools involved hundreds of client engagements with many thousands of executives and senior managers.

We helped compute possible futures in industries ranging from automotive to aerospace, electronics to semiconductors, chemicals to pharmaceuticals, to consumer goods and services, and to publishers' offerings. These engagements always addressed a range of "What if?" questions. These questions could be informed by data but not answered because the futures being considered did not exist.

The teams addressing these questions were multi-disciplinary, typically representing marketing, engineering, manufacturing, finance, sales, and customer support. They formulated models of the phenomena relevant to their questions, debated assumptions, framed scenarios, and explored the futures of interest.

In the process, there were many model-based predictions. The teams did not expect that their actual future would conform to these predictions. Instead, they provided glimpses into what *might* happen and the conditions under which these possible futures were likely to emerge. This provided them with various model-based insights into their offerings and markets.

In the process, team members learned about each other's perspectives of the problem being addressed, what variables really mattered to them, and what tradeoffs they saw as central. In this way, the models and tools spanned the boundaries among the disciplines. People left these sessions with much richer team mental models.

EPILOGUE

We aspired to be the Microsoft for business strategy tools, roughly analogous to Windows and Office (Word, PowerPoint, and Excel). We did not anticipate the level of service that clients would expect. They wanted our expertise in using the tools as applied to their problems. They wanted us, as expensive as we were, to decrease their cost of success.

As noted earlier, when the Internet bubble burst in 2000, our impressive order book for software and consulting crumbled. Clients decided to wait and see how things played out. This created a significant gap in our financial projections. Fortunately, some new businesses from former clients emerged to fill the gap. This led to the bigger pictures described in the upcoming chapters.

FURTHER READING

Rouse, W.B. (1994). *Best Laid Plans*. New York: Prentice-Hall.

Rouse, W.B. (1996) *Start Where You Are: Matching Your Strategy to your Marketplace*. San Francisco: Jossey-Bass.

Rouse, W.B. (1998). *Don't Jump to Solutions: Thirteen Delusions That Undermine Strategic Thinking*. San Francisco: Jossey-Bass.

Rouse, W.B. (2001). *Essential Challenges of Strategic Management*. New York: Wiley.

7

Enterprise Transformation

DOI: 10.4324/9781003365549-7

PROLOGUE

I returned to Georgia Tech as the Chair of the School of Industrial and Systems Engineering (ISyE) in October 2001. This is the number one ranked program in the field, as of this writing, for over 30 years. Fortunately, this ranking did not suffer during my four years as Chair.

As discussed earlier, I felt that the program needed a tangible artifact – rather than just sets of equations – much as aeronautical engineering has airplanes, missiles, and satellites, civil engineering has bridges and roads, electrical engineering has computer hardware and electronics, and mechanical engineering has automobiles and factories.

During my interview for this position, I proclaimed that our artifact was the enterprise as a complex system, rather than as a set of functional siloes, as business schools are organized. Several key members of the search committee liked this idea. Many faculty members did not. Apparently, it sounded too much like engineering rather than mathematics. Nevertheless, I got the job.

By 2003, I had replaced the ISyE Newsletter with a full-fledged magazine, *Engineering Enterprise*. I was interviewed by *Industrial Engineering* magazine in 2004 in a piece entitled "Embracing the Enterprise." By mid-2004, I had secured a $5 million gift from Michael Tennenbaum to form the Tennenbaum Institute (TI), focused on enterprise transformation.

By 2005, I had become increasingly frustrated by several senior faculty members' dissatisfaction with the enterprise theme. I had not asked them to embrace this theme. However, they did not like another major player on the intellectual stage. I stepped down from school Chair in the summer of 2005 to become full-time executive director of the Tennenbaum Institute.

I quickly moved to establish thought leadership. Recruiting top academics and executives as contributing authors, *Organization Simulation* was published in 2005 and *Enterprise Transformation* in 2006, both published by Wiley. The *Tennenbaum Institute Series on Enterprise Systems* was launched in 2007 and published by IOS Press in Amsterdam.

Five edited books in the series addressed the topics of work, workflow, and information systems (2007), enterprise mobility (2008), engineering the system of healthcare delivery (2010), complex socio-technical systems (2012), and manufacturing in a global enterprise (2012). TI was steadily achieving increased visibility.

The Georgia Tech leadership at the time TI was founded was immensely supportive. A new leadership team arrived in 2009. Frustrated with this new senior leadership, I resigned as TI executive director in 2011. Soon eligible for a full pension, I retired from Tech in August 2012 and moved to Stevens Institute of Technology as Alexander Crombie Humphreys Chair in September 2012.

In this chapter, I tell the story of what we learned about enterprise transformation during the decade 2001–12. These lessons heavily influenced my more recent endeavors during 2012–22. I explain how in later chapters.

CHALLENGES OF INNOVATION

In earlier chapters, I considered markets and competitors in terms of product and service offerings. I addressed technology adoption to enhance these offerings and gain competitive advantages. Successful adoption of the model-based approaches in these chapters can be helped or hindered by the nature of the enterprise.

Companies such as Kodak, Polaroid, Digital, Xerox, Motorola, and Nokia developed technologies that were potential market innovations. However, these technologies remained on the shelf while these companies tried to continue milking the cash cows of their existing offerings. Competitors beat them to the marketplace, and these companies are now mere shadows of their former selves.

It is very difficult to successfully innovate when new offerings make obsolete your current offerings. It can require the transformation of your enterprise. However, as noted earlier, it has been suggested that transforming an enterprise is akin to rewiring a building while the power is on. How can we design and develop a transformed enterprise while also avoiding operational disruptions and unintended consequences in the process? To address this question, we need a deeper understanding of the notion of enterprise transformation.

Our earlier studies have led us to formulate a qualitative theory:

> Enterprise transformation is driven by experienced and/or anticipated value deficiencies that result in significantly redesigned and/or new work processes as determined by management's decision making abilities, limitations, and inclinations, all in the context of the social networks of management in particular and the enterprise in general.

CONTEXT OF TRANSFORMATION

Enterprise transformation occurs in – and is at least partially driven by – the external context of the economy and markets. The economy affects markets that, in turn, affect enterprises. Of course, it is not really crisply hierarchical in that the economy can directly affect enterprises, e.g., via regulation and taxation. The key point is that the nature and extent of transformation are context dependent, as shown in Figure 7.1.

For public sector enterprises, the term "constituency" can replace the term "market." Financially oriented metrics also have to be changed to

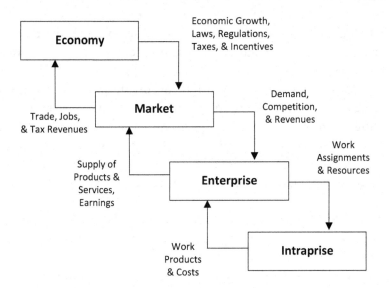

FIGURE 7.1
Context of Transformation.

reflect battles won, diseases cured, etc. I will occasionally draw parallels between private and public sector enterprises; however, full treatment of these parallels is one theme in Chapter 10.

There is also an internal context of transformation – the "intraprise." Work assignments are pursued via work processes and yield work products, incurring costs. Values and culture, reward and recognition systems, individual and team competencies, and leadership are woven throughout the intraprise. These factors usually have strong impacts on an enterprise's inclinations and abilities to pursue transformation.

MODELING THE ENTERPRISE

Enterprise transformation occurs in the external context noted above. The enterprise, with its internal strengths and weaknesses, and external opportunities and threats, operates within this broader external context. Possibilities for transformation are defined by the relationships between the enterprise and this context.

Relationships among the elements of the enterprise system are as follows. Inputs affect both work processes and enterprise state. For example, input resources (e.g., people, technology, and investment) affect both how work is done and how well it is done. As another example, input market conditions (e.g., demand and competition) affect the quality and pricing of products and services.

The concept of "state" is central to the theory of enterprise transformation. The state of a system is the set of variables and their values that enable assessing where the system is and projecting where it is going. We tend to think that financial statements define the state of an enterprise as a system. However, financial variables are usually insufficient to project the future of an enterprise, and a deeper characterization of the state is needed.

Output is derived from the evolving state of the enterprise. For example, revenues can be determined from the number of units of products or services sold and the prices of these offerings. Determining profits requires also knowing the costs of providing offerings. Units sold relate, at least in part, to customer satisfaction as determined by product and service functionality, quality, and price, all relative to competing offerings.

The construct of "value" is central to the arguments that follow. The value of the enterprise is traditionally viewed as its market capitalization, i.e., share price times the number of outstanding shares. Share price is traditionally conceptualized as the net present value of future enterprise's free cash flows, i.e., revenues minus costs. This view of value is often characterized as shareholder value.

From this perspective, state variables such as revenues, costs, quality, and price determine value. These variables are themselves determined by both work processes and architectural relationships among processes. Inputs such as investments of resources affect work processes. Coming full circle, the value of projected outputs influences how input resources are attracted and allocated.

Enterprises can be characterized in terms of the elements of domains, processes, states, work, and value. It is important to note that value, for example, in terms of unit prices, will depend on the competing offerings from other enterprises. Similarly, the importance of any set of military objectives secured depends on the objectives secured by adversaries. Thus, as noted earlier, knowledge of context is essential to understanding enterprises as systems.

It could be argued that all of these elements are simply intermediate surrogates for shareholder value; hence, shareholder value is the central construct. On the other hand, it is very difficult to argue that shareholder value, as traditionally defined, is the sole driver of enterprise transformation. For many types of enterprises, shareholder value is the ultimate measure of success, but other forces, such as markets, technologies, and the economy, often drive change.

Many fundamental changes address value from the perspective of customers and, to a much lesser extent, suppliers and employees. According to Peter Drucker, "The purpose of a business is to create a customer." Thus, for example, while loss of market share and subsequent decreasing stock market valuation can be viewed as end effects in themselves, they also may be seen as symptoms of the declining value of products and services as perceived by customers.

QUALITATIVE THEORY

Succinctly, experienced or expected value deficiencies drive enterprise transformation initiatives. Deficiencies are defined relative to both current enterprise states and expected states. Expectations may be based on the extrapolation of past enterprise states. They may also be based on perceived opportunities to pursue expanded markets, new constituencies, technologies, etc. Thus, deficiencies may be perceived for both reactive and proactive reasons.

Transformation initiatives involve addressing what work is undertaken by the enterprise and how this work is accomplished. The work of the enterprise ultimately affects the state of the enterprise, which is reflected, in part, in the enterprise's financial statements, balanced scorecard assessment, or the equivalent. Other important elements of the enterprise state might include market advantage, brand image, employee and customer satisfaction, and so on. In general, the state of the enterprise does not include variables internal to work processes.

This is due to the fact that we only need state estimates sufficient to enable explaining, predicting, and/or controlling future states of the system. To illustrate, the state of an aircraft is usually defined in terms of its location, speed, attitude, etc., but not the current RPM of its fuel pumps, air flow in the cabin, and electron charge of its LED displays. Similarly, the state of an enterprise does not include the current locations of all salespeople, ambient temperatures in each of its factories, the water flow in the restrooms, etc. Were we not able to define state at a higher level of aggregation and abstraction, the complexity of modeling airplanes or enterprises would be intractable.

VALUE DEFICIENCIES DRIVE TRANSFORMATION

More specifically, enterprise transformation is driven by perceived value deficiencies relative to needs and/or expectations due to:

- Experienced or expected downside losses of value, e.g., declining enterprise revenues and/or profits.
- Experienced or expected failures to meet projected or promised upside gains of value, e.g., failures to achieve anticipated enterprise growth.
- Desires to achieve new levels of value, e.g., via exploitation of market and/or technological opportunities.

In all of these cases, there are often beliefs that change will enable remediation of such value deficiencies. Change can range from business process improvement to more fundamental enterprise transformation.

WORK PROCESSES ENABLE TRANSFORMATION

In general, there are three broad ways to approach value deficiencies, all of which involve consideration of the work of the enterprise:

- Improve how work is currently performed, e.g., reduce variability.
- Perform current work differently, e.g., web-enabled customer service.
- Perform different work, e.g., outsource manufacturing and focus on service.

The first choice is basically business process improvement. This choice is less likely to be transformative than the other two choices. The second choice often involves operational changes that can be transformative depending on the scope of changes. The third choice is most likely to result in transforming the enterprise. This depends, however, on how resources are redeployed. Liquidation, in itself, is not necessarily transformative.

The need to focus on work processes is well recognized. Reengineered and lean processes have been goals in many transformative initiatives. Indeed, a focus on processes may, at least initially, require the transformation of management's thinking about an enterprise. The extent to which this subsequently transforms the enterprise depends on the extent of changes and success in their implementation.

Transformation can also involve relationships among processes, not just individual work processes in and of themselves. These relationships are often framed in terms of an "architecture." It is common to express architectures in terms of multiple "views." The operational view is a description of the activities, operational elements, and information flows required to support enterprise operations. The technical view is a set of rules defining the interactions and interdependencies of system elements to assure compatibility and satisfaction of requirements. The system view describes the physical connections, locations, key nodes, etc., needed to support enterprise functions.

Transformation of work processes inherently must affect the operational view of the architecture. Changes in this view are likely to affect the technical and systems views. In contrast, changes in system and/or technical views that do not change operational views do not, by definition, change work processes. Hence, these types of changes may improve processes but do not transform the enterprise.

Changing the tasks and activities of the enterprise, by themselves, relates to business process improvement. In contrast, changing the purpose, objectives, and/or functions of the enterprise is more likely to be transformational. Such changes may, of course, cause tasks and activities to then change. Thus, change at any level in the hierarchy is likely to cause changes at lower levels.

Ultimately, one could liquidate the enterprise and redeploy its financial and perhaps physical assets in other ventures. However, it is difficult to characterize this as transformation. Thus, there is a point at which the change is sufficiently substantial to conclude that the enterprise has been eliminated rather than transformed.

Finally, it is useful to note that a multi-level enterprise architecture provides a broader view of the enterprise in that it includes elements of the context noted above. This broader view is often essential to addressing change, while other elements of the context are changing as well. The changing payment system in healthcare provides an interesting illustration of providers pursuing transformation while the external context is changing and not always predictably.

MANAGEMENT DECISION MAKING

Value deficiencies and work processes define the problem of enterprise transformation – one should recognize and/or anticipate deficiencies and then redesign work processes to remediate these deficiencies. To fully understand transformation, however, we need to understand both the problem and the problem solvers. Thus, the characterization of management decision making is central to our overall theory.

Mintzberg's classic paper, as well as more recent works, serves to shatter the myth of the manager as a coolly analytical strategist, completely focused on optimizing shareholder value using leading-edge methods and tools. Simon articulates the concept of "satisficing," whereby managers find solutions that are "good enough" rather than optimal. Another important factor is the organizational environment that can be rife with delusions that undermine strategic thinking as I discussed in Chapter 6.

This somewhat skeptical view of management decision making ignores several important aspects of human decision making. Managers' expertise and intuitions and abilities to respond effectively in a blink can be key to success, especially in recognizing what is really happening in an enterprise. Managers' roles as leaders, rather than problem solvers and decision makers, are also central to transformation.

Summarizing, the problem of transformation (i.e., value deficiencies prompting a redesign of processes) combines with the nature of the problem solvers addressing transformation, as well as their organizations, to determine whether transformation is addressed, how it is addressed, and how well desired outcomes are achieved. The key point is that explanations of any particular instance of transformation will depend on the situation faced by the enterprise, the nature of the particular managers leading the enterprise, and the social structure of the enterprise.

In summary, transformation is driven by value deficiencies and involves examining and changing work processes. This examination involves consideration of how changes are likely to affect the future state of the enterprise. Potential impacts on enterprise states are assessed in terms of value consequences. Projected consequences can, and should, influence how investments of attention and resources are allocated. The problem-solving and decision-making abilities of management, as well as the social context, influence how and how well all of this happens.

ENDS, MEANS, AND SCOPE OF TRANSFORMATION

As shown in Figure 7.2, there is a wide range of ways to pursue transformation. The ends of transformation can range from greater cost efficiencies, to enhanced market perceptions, to new product and service offerings, and to fundamental changes in markets. The means can range from upgrading people's skills, to redesigning business practices, to significant infusions of technology, and to fundamental changes in strategy. The scope of transformation can range from work

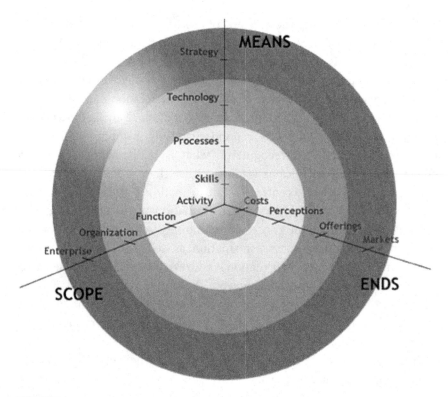

FIGURE 7.2
Transformation Framework.

activities, to business functions, to overall organizations, and to the enterprise as a whole.

The dimensions of this framework have provided a useful categorization of a broad range of case studies of enterprise transformation. Considering the transformation of markets, Amazon leveraged IT to redefine book buying, while Wal-Mart leveraged IT to redefine the retail industry. In these two instances at least, it can be argued that Amazon and Wal-Mart just grew; they did not transform. Nevertheless, their markets were transformed. The US Department of Defense's (DoD) effort to move to capabilities-based acquisition (e.g., buying airlifts rather than airplanes) has the potential to transform both DoD and its suppliers.

Illustrations of transformation of offerings include UPS moving from being a package delivery company to a global supply chain management provider, IBM's transition from manufacturing to services, Motorola moving from battery eliminators to radios to cell phones, and CNN redefining news delivery. Examples of transformation of perceptions include Dell repositioning computer buying, Starbucks repositioning coffee purchases, and Victoria's Secret repositioning lingerie buying. The many instances of transforming business operations include Lockheed Martin merging three aircraft companies, Newell Rubbermaid resuscitating numerous home products companies, and Interface adopting green business practices.

The costs and risks of transformation increase as the endeavor moves farther from the center, i.e., towards changing markets via changing strategies across the whole enterprise. Initiatives focused on cost efficiencies and upgrading skills for targeted work activities will typically involve well-known and mature methods and tools from industrial engineering and operations management. In contrast, initiatives towards the perimeter will often require substantial changes in products, services, channels, etc., as well as associated large investments.

It is important to note that successful transformations in the outer band of these three dimensions are likely to require significant investments in the inner bands also. In general, any level of transformation requires consideration of all subordinate levels. Thus, for example, successfully changing the market's perceptions of an enterprise's offerings is likely to also require enhanced operational excellence to underpin the new image being sought. As another illustration, significant changes in strategies often require new processes for decision making, e.g., for R&D investments.

VALUE PERSPECTIVES

Elaborating on earlier value-centered arguments, there are basically four alternative perspectives that tend to drive the needs for transformation:

- Value Opportunities: the lure of greater success via market and/or technology opportunities prompts transformation initiatives.
- Value Threats: the danger of anticipated failure due to market and/or technology threats prompts transformation initiatives.
- Value Competition: other players' transformation initiatives prompt recognition that transformation is necessary for continued success.

- Value Crises: steadily declining market performance, cash flow problems, etc., prompt recognition that transformation is necessary to survive.

The perspectives driven by external opportunities and threats often allow pursuing transformation long before it is forced on management, increasing the chances of having resources to invest in these pursuits, leveraging internal strengths, and mitigating internal weaknesses. In contrast, the perspectives driven by external competitors' initiatives and internally caused crises typically lead to the need for transformation being recognized much later and, consequently, often forced on management by corporate parents, equity markets, or other investors. Such reactive perspectives on transformation often lead to failures.

WORK PERSPECTIVES

Transformation initiatives driven by external opportunities and threats tend to adopt strategy-oriented approaches such as:

- Markets Targeted, e.g., pursuing global markets such as emerging markets, or pursuing vertical markets such as aerospace and defense.
- Market Channels Employed, e.g., adding web-based sales of products and services such as automobiles, consumer electronics, and computers.
- Value Proposition, e.g., moving from selling unbundled products and services to providing integrated solutions for information technology management.
- Offerings Provided, e.g., changing the products and services provided, perhaps by private labeling of outsourced products and focusing on support services.

On the other hand, transformation initiatives driven by competitors' initiatives and internal crises tend to adopt operations-oriented approaches including:

- Supply Chain Restructuring, e.g., simplifying supply chains, negotiating just-in-time relationships, developing collaborative information systems.

- Outsourcing and Offshoring, e.g., contracting out manufacturing, information technology support; employing low-wage, high-skill labor from other countries.
- Process Standardization, e.g., enterprise-wide standardization of processes for product and process development, R&D, finance, personnel, etc.
- Process Reengineering, e.g., identification, design, and deployment of value-driven processes; identification and elimination of non-value creating activities.
- Web-Enabled Processes, e.g., online, self-support systems for customer relationship management, inventory management, etc.

It is essential to note, however, that no significant transformation initiative can rely solely on either of these sets of approaches. Strategy-oriented initiatives must eventually pay serious attention to operations. Similarly, operations-oriented initiatives must at least validate existing strategies or run the risk of becoming very good at something they should not be doing at all.

The above approaches drive reconsideration of work processes. Processes are replaced or redesigned to align with strategy choices. Operational approaches enhance the effectiveness and efficiency of processes. Of course, the possibilities of changing work processes depend greatly on the internal context of transformation. Leadership is the key, but rewards and recognition, competencies, and so on also have strong impacts on success. Social networks enormously affect the implementation of change.

Work processes can be enhanced (by acceleration, task improvement, and output improvement), streamlined (by elimination of tasks), eliminated (by outsourcing), and invented (by creation of new processes). An example of acceleration is the use of workflow technology to automate information flow between process steps or tasks. An illustration of task improvement is the use of decision-aiding technology to improve human performance on a given process task (e.g., enabling consideration of more options).

Output improvement might involve, for example, decreasing process variability. Streamlining could involve transferring tasks to others (e.g., transferring customer service queries to other customers who have addressed similar questions). Elimination involves curtailing processes, e.g., Amazon created online bookstores, thus eliminating the need for bookstore-related processes in their business. Invention involves creating new processes, e.g., Dell created innovative build-to-order processes.

COMPUTATIONAL THEORY

The qualitative theory elaborated above provides a well-founded explanation of enterprise transformation as well as a framework for organizing case studies and best practices. However, it does not enable quantitative predictions of the outcomes of transformation and, in particular, the impacts of alternative strategy choices.

These choices include predicting better, learning faster, and acting faster. Predicting better decreases uncertainties about future states of market demands and competitors' offerings. Learning faster implies that knowledge gained is more quickly incorporated into enterprise competencies. Acting faster quickly turns predictions and knowledge into practice. These three strategy choices each require investments.

We wanted to know the conditions under which these investments make sense. The key elements of the computational theory included the following:

- Management: represents decisions to allocate resources to remediate value deficiencies and maximize expected utility.
- Production: represents mapping of resources, including labor, to products and services over time.
- Market: represents mapping from products and services to value that leads to revenues, profits, and cash flows over time.
- Social Network: represents allocation of human attention to deploy resources, including the provision of information for decision making.

We translated the relationships among these elements into a set of equations to enable a computational theory of enterprise transformation. Thus, the enterprise and the marketplace were represented by a set of interacting equations, which we used to explore which transformation initiatives are most useful under which particular sets of conditions.

The computational theory predicted that companies will transform their enterprise by some combination of predicting better, learning faster, and acting faster, as long as the market is sufficiently predictable to reasonably expect that transformation will improve the market value that the company can provide. If this expectation is unreasonable, then companies will sit tight and preserve resources until the market becomes more fathomable.

Put simply, if the market is highly volatile and customers are very discriminating, then the impacts of investments in transformation are likely to be negative because it is so difficult to hit a moving target in a turbulent environment. Companies sitting tight and preserving resources are often observed when the economy is weak, the market is hypercompetitive, and/or government policy is uncertain. In such situations, the computational model tended to show that the optimal strategy was to do nothing.

The computational theory was premised on the notion that companies make transformation decisions in response to the dynamic situations in which they find themselves. These decisions are affected by both what the company knows (or perceives) and the company's abilities to predict, learn, and act. Indeed, decisions to transform abilities to predict, learn, and act, reflect desires to fundamentally change the company's overall ability to create market value. In this way, transformation decisions can enhance a company's abilities to address the ongoing and anticipated fundamental changes needed for success in dynamic markets.

This does not imply that everything will change. Instead, it means that everything needs to be considered in terms of how things consistently fit together, function smoothly, and provide high-value outcomes. This may be daunting but is entirely feasible. The key point is that one may not be able to transform value propositions without considering how the delivery enterprise itself should be transformed.

I hasten to note that, at this point, I am only addressing what is likely to have to change, not how the changes can be accomplished. In particular, the success of transformation initiatives depends on gaining the support of stakeholders, managing their perceptions and expectations, and sustaining fundamental change. Leading initiatives where these factors play major roles requires competencies in vision, leadership, strategy, planning, culture, collaboration, and teamwork. The marshaling of these competencies and their deployment can be orchestrated by adopting a human-centered design perspective.

CONCLUSIONS

The fundamental transformation of a large enterprise is very difficult. Data on the Fortune 500 reported in *The Economist* supports this assertion:

- During 1956–81, an average of 24 firms dropped out of the Fortune 500 list every year. This amounts to a 120% turnover in that 25-year period.
- During 1982–2006, an average of 40 firms dropped out of the Fortune 500 list every year. This amounts to a 200% turnover in the more recent 25-year period.

Thus, successful enterprise transformation is not only very difficult, it is becoming more difficult, and the failure rate is very high.

The extent of this difficulty is far from new. In *Start Where You Are*, I summarized the changes addressed by roughly 200 enterprises over two centuries. Many of these enterprises tried to avoid being victims of "creative destruction," but almost all of them eventually failed. More contemporary case stories, with similar results, are discussed in *Enterprise Transformation*.

Most enterprises eventually fail, but not everyone fails. *Enterprise Transformation* discusses four detailed case studies of success at Lockheed Martin, Newell Rubbermaid, Reebok, and UPS, in terms of drivers of transformation, approach to transformation, and elements of transformation. The key elements of transformation in these four success stories were a focus on the customer, emphasis on operational efficiency, addressing the enterprise culture, and results-driven execution.

At the beginning of this chapter, I used Kodak, Polaroid, Digital, Xerox, Motorola, and Nokia as examples of companies that did not change and did not remediate their emerging value deficiencies. All of these companies had periods of great success, when revenues, profits, and share prices were soaring. Then they were overtaken by creative destruction. These case studies are elaborated on in *Failure Management*.

From a broad perspective, creative destruction is a powerful, positive force. New value propositions, often enabled by new technologies, led by new, innovative competitors take markets away from established players. Jobs are created. The economy grows. People can, therefore, afford cars, TVs, smartphones, etc.

The story is not as positive for the incumbents. They are under constant pressure. They have to face the dilemma of running the company they have while they try to become the company they want. But, the company they have is usually consuming all the money and talent. They need to address the balance between investing in getting better at what they are already doing versus investing in doing new things.

It is very difficult to achieve this balance. Most of the stakeholders are strongly committed to the status quo. They need resources and attention to keep the status quo functioning. Many of the stakeholders in the future have yet to arrive. Consequently, they are not very demanding. Creating a sense of urgency is usually essential to addressing this stalemate.

Various pundits express this in the sense of needing a "burning platform." Rather than employing physical danger or the risks of imminent demise, one can use computational models to explore possible futures, both those that are desirable and those to be avoided. This can enable identifying leading indicators of both positive and negative changes. The result can be stories of change that, hopefully, everyone can understand and find compelling. I discuss examples of this approach in Chapter 8.

EPILOGUE

My second full-time appointment at Georgia Tech was 2001–12. My first appointment was 1981–88. In between, I had an adjunct appointment while I built and managed Search Technology, Inc., and Enterprise Support Systems, Inc. The leadership at Tech was always supportive of my entrepreneurial ventures. I felt embraced by the Tech community during my 31 years in Atlanta. I certainly benefited from many faculty colleagues and numerous Tech students and alumni whom I employed. The quality of the students from engineering and computing was superb.

Atlanta was a good place to start and grow businesses. A large number of small technology companies led to frequent networking opportunities as, seemingly, everyone was trying to learn technology-based entrepreneurship together. The quality of life and the costs of living in Atlanta were very attractive to prospective employees. Admittedly, the traffic was always rather overwhelming, and car travel was the only reasonable choice. However, all in all, Atlanta was a good place to learn about business. In the following chapters, I discuss where these experiences took me.

FURTHER READING

Drucker, P. (1954). *The Practice of Management*. New York: Harper.

Rouse, W.B. (1996). *Start Where You Are: Matching Your Strategy to Your Marketplace*. San Francisco: Jossey-Bass.

Rouse, W.B. (1998). *Don't Jump to Solutions: Thirteen Delusions That Undermine Strategic Thinking*. San Francisco: Jossey-Bass.

Rouse, W.B. (2001). *Essential Challenges of Strategic Management*. New York: Wiley.

Rouse, W.B. (Ed.).(2006). *Enterprise Transformation: Understanding and Enabling Fundamental Change*. Hoboken: John Wiley.

Rouse, W.B. (2007). *People and Organizations: Explorations of Human-Centered Design*. New York: Wiley.

Rouse, W.B. (2021). *Failure Management: Malfunctions of Technologies, Organizations, and Society*. Oxford, UK: Oxford University Press.

Rouse, W.B., & Boff, K.R. (Eds.). (2005). *Organizational Simulation: From Modeling and Simulation to Games and Entertainment*. New York: Wiley.

8

Health and Education

DOI: 10.4324/9781003365549-8

PROLOGUE

As I was contemplating retirement from Georgia Tech in the summer of 2012, I called Dinesh Verma with a question. Dinesh was Dean of the School of Systems and Enterprises (SSE), as well as Executive Director of the Systems Engineering Research Center (SERC), both at Stevens Institute of Technology. I had a contract with SERC and wanted to continue this research but would no longer be at a SERC university. Was there any way to continue?

Dinesh responded immediately that he had a better idea. They were currently in the search process for a new Alexander Crombie Humphreys Chair in SSE. Might I be interested in this position? I traveled to Stevens, interviewed, and negotiated an amazingly attractive offer. I accepted and moved to the campus in Hoboken, New Jersey, directly across the Hudson River from Manhattan. The view of New York City was amazing.

I was also appointed founding Director of the Center for Complex Systems and Enterprises (CCSE). Lockheed Martin provided a generous grant to launch the center. There was a steady stream of SERC funding. We also attracted funding from the Centers for Medicare & Medicaid Services and Robert Wood Johnson Foundation. I discuss these research projects in this chapter.

Stevens was a different world than Georgia Tech, the University of Illinois, and my other university experiences. It was small with only a few thousand students. The organizational infrastructure was rather limited. Research management often involved a bit of sleuthing to determine who was authorized to approve what. People were well-intended and supportive, but not always fully competent.

Hoboken is a city of 50,000 people living in 1 square mile on what was originally an island. It was claimed to have the most pubs per capita in any city. There were 160 restaurants. It is a very walkable city, and I did not need a car, which would have required expensive monthly parking fees. Relying on public transportation meant frequent subway or ferry trips to Manhattan. Initially, at least, this seemed like fun.

Metropolitan New York City is a very expensive place to live. Rents are astonishingly high. I moved every year, seeking lower rent for acceptable quality lodging. Stevens was paying me well, but it bothered me to be paying so much. I remember being in Manhattan one morning and seeing a sign outside a parking garage, "Early bird special – $35 per hour."

The culture in Hoboken was dominated by Manhattan. Every morning, many thousands of Hoboken residents streamed to the city by ferry or subway. They all streamed back in the evening. I frequently ate at pubs, chatting with whoever happened to be next to me. They invariably worked in the financial industry, often at hedge funds. I ceased to be interested in the art of making money for its own sake.

I was spending roughly one week per month in Washington, DC, where my research sponsors were and my National Academy activities were centered. By late 2016, I decided to relocate to Washington. This did not please the senior leadership of Stevens, despite the easy and frequent Amtrak connections between DC and Hoboken. I am getting ahead of this story and will return to it later.

HEALTH AND WELLNESS

I focus on the health and well-being of people in this chapter. I consider how health services are provided in the US delivery ecosystem. This highly fragmented system presents challenges to providers, payers, and regulators at local, state, and federal levels. Not surprisingly, the emphasis of this chapter is on model-based approaches to support decision making.

This emphasis carried over from the experiences discussed in Chapters 5–7, with three very important differences. First, we became less concerned with enterprise revenues and profits and more focused on effective and affordable social services. Second, our purview moved from individual enterprises to broader public–private enterprises. Third, we developed a concept for a policy flight simulator, which I introduce in this chapter and elaborate in Chapter 9.

Two questions drove the six case studies discussed in this section. First, how can innovative pilot studies, involving perhaps 500–1,000 patients, be scaled for delivery to hundreds of thousands of patients? The focus of the case studies discussed here included diabetes, heart disease, Alzheimer's disease, and transition care for complex elderly patients.

The second question concerned broad enterprise-level issues. How is the health ecosystem of New York City likely to evolve in the next decade or two? How can the overall health of a broad population be maintained? How is technology likely to drive the quality and costs of health? Addressing such questions requires ambitious modeling efforts.

These scaling and enterprise issues are far from new. They have long been addressed via empirical studies, advisory boards, and other traditional mechanisms. I have addressed these issues computationally. Possible futures are computed for alternative current investment decisions. We compute what might happen and the conditions under which possible futures are likely.

DELIVERY ECOSYSTEM

There are many stakeholders involved in providing health, education, and social services in the USA. There are inherent difficulties accessing these services. As shown in Figure 8.1, the ecosystem is highly fragmented, often resulting in low-quality, expensive services. Equity of services is also a major issue, with social determinants of health having enormous impacts.

Our approach employs a framework we have developed for modeling complex social enterprises that I discuss in Chapter 9. This framework addresses the physical, human, economic, and social phenomena underlying complex ecosystems. This multi-level framework provides the basis for integrating different types of computational models to explore policy alternatives.

The people level is usually agent-based, laced with both decision theory and behavioral economics. The process level is represented as networks of flows, and resulting queues, as well as flows of information. The organizational level involves the microeconomics of resource allocation,

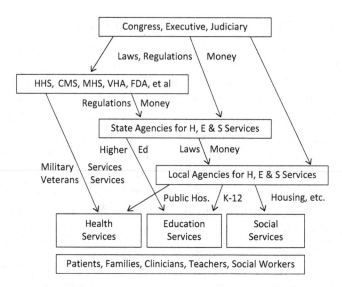

FIGURE 8.1

Fragmented US Service Delivery System.

again laced with both decision theory and behavioral economics. The level of society involves the macroeconomics of policy. The resulting multi-level model is typically embedded in an interactive visualization that enables experimentation.

At the people level, central phenomena include establishing a route through the many needed services. People may balk (not become patients) or renege (drop out of treatment) along the route, due to delay times and other factors.

Process-level phenomena include getting appointments for each service in the route. Delays between services can be characterized by weeks. Delays are highly affected by capacity constraints. Processes also involve the flow of information among service providers. Inefficiencies in the flow of information can foster inefficiencies in the flow of patients to services.

At the organization level, capacity constraints are due to investment policies, as well as the availability of personnel. Organizations, not surprisingly, tend to invest in capacities needed to provide services that are highly reimbursed. Thus, for example, cancer, cardio, and ortho surgery services are typically better provisioned than chronic disease management and mental health.

On the level of society, investment policies are related to payer reimbursement policies for different services. This level also relates to how value is defined. Healthy people not only have lower healthcare costs, they also typically work, earn incomes, pay taxes, etc. Thus, society benefits from a healthy population far in excess of the lower healthcare costs. Fragmentation at the highest level undermines accounting for the full benefits of population health.

SCALING INNOVATION

The three case studies in this section concern computational models for studying the issues associated with scaling successful pilot studies or randomized clinical trials to broad adoption. In general, inefficiencies not visible with a few hundred patients can become glaring for hundreds of thousands of patients.

Emory Prevention and Wellness

This case study addressed the employee prevention and wellness program of Emory University. The application of the multi-level model focused on the roughly 700 people in this cohort and their risks of diabetes mellitus (DM) and coronary heart disease (CHD). Each person's risk of each disease was calculated using DM and CHD risk models from the medical literature, using initial individual assessments of blood pressure, fasting glucose level, etc. Subsequent assessment data were used to estimate annual risk changes as a function of the initial risks of each disease.

The model of this healthcare delivery enterprise included the four levels of ecosystem, organization, process, and people. Each level introduced a corresponding conceptual set of issues and decisions for both the payer and provider. In this case, the Human Resources Department of Emory University (HR) was the payer responsible for healthcare costs for university employees, while the Predictive Health Institute (PHI) was the provider focused on the prevention and maintenance of employee health.

The ecosystem level allowed decision makers to test different combinations of policies from the perspective of HR. For instance, this level determined the allocation of payments to PHI based on a hybrid capitated and pay-for-outcome formula. It also involved choices of parameters such as projected healthcare inflation rate, general economy inflation rate, and discount rate that affect the economic valuation of the prevention and wellness program. One of the greatest concerns of HR was achieving a satisfactory return on investment (ROI) on any investments in prevention and wellness.

The concerns at the organization level included the economic sustainability of PHI – their revenue had to be equal to or greater than their costs. To achieve sustainability, PHI had to appropriately design its operational processes and rules. Two issues were central. What risk levels should be used to stratify the participant population? What assessment and coaching processes should be employed for each stratum of the population? Other organization-level considerations included the growth rate of the participant population, the age ranges targeted for growth, and the program duration before participants were moved to "maintenance."

The process level represented the daily operations of PHI. Participants visited PHI every 6–12 months. Seven health partners employed by PHI performed assessments, worked with participants to set health goals, and performed follow-up calls or emails to monitor participants and encourage them to follow their plan. All of these activities were captured at the process level. The costs of these activities were aggregated and reflected at the organization level as the costs of running PHI.

The people level was the replication of the actual population of PHI participants. Over a three-year period, roughly 700 participants joined this prevention and wellness program. Each of them had various assessment measurements recorded such as blood pressure, fasting glucose level, etc. – because PHI was, in part, a research project, approximately 2,000 variables were measured at each assessment encounter. Each participant was instantiated in the model as an agent. Based on the assessment measurements, the risk of developing DM or CHD was computed for each agent. Then, total healthcare costs were estimated for their remaining life based on their risk level for each disease. The reduced amount of aggregated total healthcare cost achieved by PHI is an ecosystem-level benefit to the HR organization.

Evaluating PHI as it was currently operating resulted in several conclusions. If Emory scaled up its current prevention and wellness program, it would yield an annual – 96% ROI – about as bad as you can get. Yet, they were achieving dramatic improvements for people with high risks of diabetes and heart disease. If we radically reorganized this program (computationally), we could achieve a 7% ROI for Emory and sustain the program. Those were the results through age 65.

If we extended the analysis to age 80, we achieved a 30% ROI. This difference is all to the benefit of the US Centers for Medicare and Medicaid Services (CMS). Thus, in principle at least, CMS should incentivize Emory to provide prevention and wellness to its employees. In general, CMS should incentivize all employers to keep people healthy so that when they enter Medicare at age 65, they are much healthier and less expensive to CMS.

To achieve this impressive ROI and stay in business, PHI had to change its business model, stratifying the population by risk levels and tailoring processes to each stratum. This included an initial low-cost, streamlined assessment, and subsequently, PHI "Lite" for low-risk participants. PHI also needed to develop a low-cost "maintenance" process to sustain reduced risks once they have been achieved. These recommendations significantly influenced the subsequent redesign of PHI.

Indiana Alzheimer's Care

This case study addressed care for patients with memory and emotional problems such as Alzheimer's disease and other related dementia. There is a substantial need to develop new scalable and sustainable brain care services to care for these patients. This care requires extensive psychosocial support, nursing care, and comprehensive patient-centered management, which strain the resources of clinicians, family caregivers, and community-based support structures. Indiana University developed such a health management program called the Aging Brain Care Medical Home (ABC) to provide the collaborative care model to 1,500 older adults in central Indiana.

In order to scale up the ABC collaborative care model to more patients and other geographical areas, it was necessary to understand what factors affect the efficiency and effectiveness of its operations and outcomes. To this end, we developed a multi-level computer simulation model of the ABC program. It was shown that scaling the program without modification would be infeasible. More broadly, the ABC simulation model served as a risk-reduction decision support tool for healthcare delivery redesign, allowing early identification of operational and redesign issues.

The ABC simulation model included elements from both agent-based and discrete-event modeling, incorporated in the overall multi-level model.

The model was used to explore different strategies for scaling up the ABC program. Results showed that as population sizes increased, economies of scale would be reached, and thus the contribution of fixed costs to the costs per member or patient would decrease. Another important finding that emerged from this study was that the impact of the ABC program on cost savings reaches a steady state after a period of several years, which was indicated by a decreasing standard error and plateaued ROIs.

In the process of conducting this study we encountered a data set for 70,000 Alzheimer's patients over several years. This allowed us to estimate transition rates among six states of health: normal, mild cognitive impairment, mild Alzheimer's, moderate Alzheimer's, severe Alzheimer's, and death. We also had data on the annual costs of care for each state.

Alzheimer's disease cannot be cured or reversed at this time. However, progression can be delayed via various interventions. We explored the impacts of delays, by varying probabilities of retaining patients in less advanced states of 0%, 5%, or 10%. Using simulation, we found that a 5%–10% increase in retaining patients in less advanced states can yield enormous annual savings of roughly 50% by year six. The percent savings increases with age because older patients die before they advance to the severe stage and need nursing home care.

This use of modeling is interesting in that we predicted the economic value of an unknown intervention. We do not know how to increase the probabilities by 5%–10%. However, we do know what it would be worth if we could develop this intervention – half the cost of Alzheimer's care in the USA. Our goal was to motivate parties who might be able to figure this out.

Penn Transition Care for Elderly Patients

The Transitional Care Model (TCM) is a proven care management approach developed by Penn Medicine that can contribute to a more person-centered, effective, and efficient response to the challenge of chronic illness, including the needs to avoid readmissions and associated penalties.

Despite TCM's proven value, it has been challenging to convince decision makers to implement this model. Success in TCM's spread has been achieved only slowly – one health system or community at a time. Among major barriers to widespread implementation are perceptions that the model has been demonstrated to work in randomized control and comparative effectiveness trials but not in the "real world," is too complex and costly, requires upfront investment which will largely benefit other providers downstream, or is not adaptable to local contextual issues.

While each of these misperceptions has been addressed through the successful translation of the TCM in a number of health systems, traditional strategies (e.g., identifying local champions, multiple meetings with decision makers) consume substantial time and are not as efficient as desired in promoting widespread scaling. Such challenges are not limited to the adoption of the TCM and addressing them could have positive impacts on the widespread adoption of evidence care throughout the US healthcare system.

To that end, the specific goal of this case study was to determine whether the use of a policy flight simulator accelerates positive decisions to implement the TCM. As indicated in earlier discussions, policy flight simulators fuse aspects of scientific analysis, engineering, social science, and visualization to provide decision makers with a more comprehensive understanding of the consequences of interventions than that provided by traditional mathematical and computational approaches. I discuss the design of these simulators in Chapter 9.

To accomplish this goal, the team conducted activities in an iterative, adaptive process. We elicited barriers and facilitators to adopting evidence-based, highly effective interventions from decision makers representing providers, payers, and purchasers. Several key insights emerged:

- The payment system is central.
- Beliefs about evidence vary; peers' actions are important.
- Research evidence is not sufficient.
- The offering must relate to "my population."

These insights caused us to realize that any investment decision of the magnitude of TCM would likely require the involvement of many stakeholders and organizations in a given healthcare system. Consequently, we elaborated our goal, namely, to determine whether the use of an innovative policy flight simulator would help healthcare decision makers (providers, payers, or purchasers) make better-informed decisions regarding the adoption of TCM and increase their confidence in a decision to adopt TCM.

Results showed that we had demonstrated the potential value of a policy flight simulator to inform decisions about adopting evidence-based interventions. The TCM simulator enabled providers and payers to project the impact of TCM on their patient populations, using their financial parameters, e.g., local wages. This increased their confidence in how this evidence-based intervention would likely impact them and decreased the tendency to dismiss evidence that the simulator shows to be well founded.

There is little, if any, doubt that TCM benefits patients across a wide range of patient demographics. Indeed, analysis of benefits by patient demographic characteristics failed to show any variation in effectiveness with these characteristics. The question addressed was the extent to which TCM would be economically attractive for any and all providers. The answer is that one size does not fit all. Benefits depend on the patient population enrolled in TCM, the extent of readmission penalties, and the nature of the provider, e.g., tertiary versus secondary care and the payment model (capitated vs. fee-for-service).

As the Medicare population grows and new payment models are deployed, providers will have to understand in depth how their practices affect the economics of their enterprise and policymakers will want to know how to anticipate those responses. Indeed, CMS will need to understand that not all providers are the same, that policies that work for one subset of the population may not work for other subsets, and which subsets of the providers or populations are most impacted. Policy flight simulators can provide such understanding before policies are deployed.

ENTERPRISE MODELS

The enterprise issues I discuss in this section are not concerned with particular diseases or types of patients. Instead, the focus is on the broad delivery enterprise, or ecosystem of enterprises, and its behavior and performance. Hospital consolidation, population health, and the impacts of technological innovation are addressed.

New York City Health Ecosystem

The Affordable Care Act (ACA) has caused a transformation in the healthcare industry. This industry involves complicated relationships among patients, physicians, hospitals, health plans, pharmaceutical companies, healthcare equipment companies, and the government. Hospitals are uncertain about how they should best respond to threats and opportunities. This is particularly relevant for hospitals located in competitive metropolitan areas such as New York City, where more than 50 hospitals are competing – many among the nation's best. Questions that arise in this uncertain environment include:

- What if we wait until the healthcare market stabilizes and only invest in operational efficiency?
- Should we merge with competing hospitals to increase negotiation power?
- Shall we only focus on acquiring physician practices in highly reimbursed diagnostic groups?

In this case study, Annie Yu and I developed a data-rich agent-based simulation model to study dynamic interactions among healthcare systems in the context of merger and acquisition (M&A) decision making. By "rich," we meant extensive rule sets and information sources, compared to traditional agent-based models. The computational model included agents' revenues and profitability (i.e., financial statements), operational performance, and resource utilization, as well as a more detailed set of objectives and decision-making rules to address a variety of what-if scenarios.

We applied our modeling approach to M&A dynamics of hospitals in New York City, informed by in-depth data on 66 hospitals in the Hospital Referral Region in the Bronx, Manhattan, and Eastern Long Island. The objective of the simulation model was to assist hospital executives to assess the impact of implementing strategic acquisition decisions at the system level. This was accomplished by simulating strategies and interactions based on real historical hospital balance sheets and operational performance data.

The outcomes of the simulation included the number of hospitals remaining in the market and frequent M&A pairs of hospitals under various settings. By varying strategy inputs and relevant parameters, the simulation was used to generate insights as to how these outcomes would change under different scenarios. The interactive visualizations complemented the simulation model by allowing non-technical users to interactively explore relevant information, to input parameter values for different scenarios, as well as to view and validate the results of the simulation model.

The results from the simulation model facilitated M&A decision making, particularly in identifying desirable acquisition targets, aggressive and capable acquirers, and frequent acquirer–target pairs. The frequencies of prevalent pairs of acquirer and target appearing under different strategies in our simulation were of particular interest. The frequency level is a relative value in that it depends on the number of strategies included and hospitals involved. A high frequency suggests a better fit and also repeated attraction.

Validation of agent-based simulations is challenging, especially for high-level strategic decision simulations. The overall model and set of visualizations were validated in two ways. From a technical perspective, we compared our simulation results with Capital IQ's hospital mergers and acquisitions' transaction dataset. Although there were a limited number of cases under our regional constraint in Capital IQ's database, the realized M&A transactions appeared in our results.

Second is the feedback from users. There were many, roughly 30, demonstrations to hospital decision makers and healthcare consultants as well as senior executives from insurance, government, foundations, etc. In total, perhaps 200 people participated in the demos, and many took the controls and tried various options. They made many suggestions, and the number of types of interactive visualizations iteratively increased.

Two predictions were of particular interest. We correctly predicted the Mt Sinai acquisition of Beth Israel. We incorrectly predicted that Mt. Sinai would acquire Staten Island University Hospital. Instead, Northwell acquired Staten Island. During a demo to Mt Sinai, we noted this prediction. A Mt. Sinai executive said that Staten Island was at the top of their list, but Northwell acted more quickly. So this prediction was not that far off.

The key value of the overall model and set of visualizations was, of course, the insights gained by the human users of this environment. For example, they may determine the conditions under which certain outcomes are likely. They can then monitor developments to see if such conditions are emerging. Thus, they know what *might* happen, even though they cannot be assured what will happen. The greatest insights are gained not only from simulation but also from interactive visualizations that enable massive data exploration.

Population Health

Population health involves the integration of health, education, and social services to keep a defined population healthy, address health challenges holistically, and assist with the realities of being mortal. The fragmentation of the US population health delivery system makes this very difficult. We pursued several questions related to population health and learning health systems:

- To what extent can upstream interventions (e.g., education and social services) decrease the incidence and progression of the disease so that the downstream savings justify the upstream investments?
- How sensitive are results to the extent of population engagement? How is engagement affected by payment mechanisms? How might social influences and social media enhance engagement?
- How valuable are the second-order impacts of population health in terms of longer, more productive lives? Are there higher-order impacts that could have significant positive or negative effects?
- To what extent does the fragmentation of delivery, payment, and regulation across local, state, and federal stakeholders undermine the effectiveness of population health offerings? If such fragmentation was not a problem, how well could population health offerings perform in terms of health outcomes and costs?

We addressed these questions in the context of the aforementioned population health enterprise. At each level, we considered innovations needed that could leverage systems science, behavioral economics, and social networking. We also considered the implications for health IT and governance. The result was an agenda for transforming population health. An overall computational model that includes the elements of this agenda is very much a work in progress.

Technology Innovation

The last four decades have seen enormous increases in healthcare costs. Specifically, *real* healthcare costs have tripled as a percent of the GDP in the period 1965–2005, with half of this growth due to technological innovation. There seems to be virtually unanimous agreement that something has to change significantly.

Technological inventions become market innovations as they increase in effectiveness and associated risks decrease. This results in increased use, which leads to increased expenditures. In parallel, increased efficiency via production learning leads to decreased cost per use, although not enough to keep up with growing use rates in healthcare. Finally, increased use yields improved care that leads to longer lives and increased chances of again employing the technology of interest. For example, the average number of hip replacements in the USA, for people who have hip replacements, is greater than two.

The concern is how to control these phenomena. More specifically, what efficiencies must be realized to steadily decrease the cost per use to offset the constantly increased number of uses and thereby enable affordable healthcare? We approached this control problem with a series of models, beginning with a very simple model and elaborating as the limits of each model become clear. The overall conclusion is that costs per use must dramatically decrease to overcome the exponential growth of the number of uses.

Summary

The six case studies discussed thus far illustrate the broad range of applicability of computational modeling to designing, developing, and deploying the future health and well-being ecosystem. Big data and interactive visualization technology have enabled great advances. The Internet of Things (IoT) and artificial intelligence (AI), in their several forms, will further advance the state of modeling and decision support.

It is easy to imagine evidence-based and intelligent support for clinicians, patients, and their families. Economic, political, and social fragmentation may be slow to fade, but model-based design will increasingly provide what users really need and desire. As has been seen with other digital technologies, the marketplace will drive adoption despite lingering fragmentation.

HEALTH ADVISOR

We were interested in how the availability of information affected clinician performance. Rahul Basole, Doug Bodner, and I developed *Health*

Advisor, an online game where players – as advisors rather than clinicians – advised simulated clients on referrals to medical specialties. They had available patients' EHRs (Electronic Health Records) and an information resource named Medfile that provided information on symptoms, likely causes, and recommended courses of action.

Making the game realistic and interesting was a challenge. We acquired a data set of people's pictures that matched US demographics with regard to age, gender, ethnicity, etc. It took some effort to generate appropriate names, e.g., there are not many elderly women named Tiffany. Pilot testing of *Health Advisor* indicated that the simulated clients were boring. My daughter, Rebecca, synthesized personalities for the clients, e.g., talkative, reticent, and ebullient.

After several pilot tests, we conducted an experiment with 48 pre-med students at Emory University. Overall results showed that people's perceptions of the usability and usefulness of information sources had a strong impact on the use of these sources, and a significant impact on their subsequent performance in diagnoses and referrals. Put simply, people who rushed through the game did very poorly by their clients.

One last evaluation was conducted by my son, Will, as a 14-year-old summer intern. He compared *Health Advisor* to seven popular online games. His 50-page report provided detailed recommendations on how to make the game more understandable, challenging, and fun. He was just the right age to conduct such a study.

It was very clear that a large percentage of students played the game as intended, carefully weighing available information to make good decisions. A smaller but significant percentage of the students just wanted to whiz through as quickly as possible. This suggests that care must be taken in interpreting experimental results from such synthetic environments.

EDUCATION

My initial forays into healthcare happened in the last year or so of my time at Georgia Tech. Members of the Tennenbaum Institute (TI) Advisory Board often asked me when I was going to address the transformation of higher education. I could not imagine anyone sponsoring that, so I soft peddled the topic. Then my CCSE Advisory Board asked me the same question. I started paying attention.

During 2014–15, I delved into higher education, trying to understand why it had replaced healthcare delivery as the poster child for runaway costs. Increases in the price of tuition and fees were far outstripping increasing healthcare costs and, by far, any increases in costs of living. My scrutiny of these phenomena resulted in *Universities as Complex Enterprises* and subsequent articles.

COMPUTATIONAL MODEL

I developed a computational economic model for research universities, shown in Figure 8.2. With its publication in *Proceedings of the National Academies of Science*, this model was made publicly available and downloaded by many universities. I developed the model to explore how research universities would address three major trends.

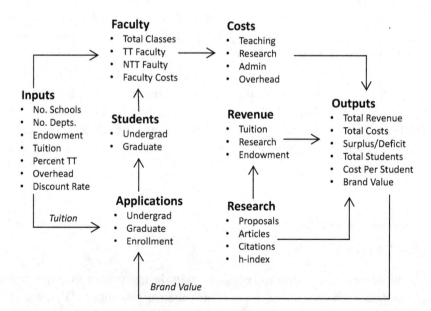

FIGURE 8.2
Economic Model of Research Universities.

This computational model is based on a thorough analysis of a wealth of data pertaining to the various aspects of a university enterprise. This includes sources of funding, alternative publication outlets, predictors of brand value (and hence, rankings), workforce structure, administrative practices, and the like.

In this model, student applications are driven by tuition and brand value. While expected degree completion time and potential job opportunities play a role, tuition and brand value dominate. Accepted students who enroll, as well as continuing students, determine the needs for classes and faculty members to teach these classes, which drives the costs of teaching. Tenure track (TT) faculty members need to pursue research to achieve tenure and promotion. They need to write proposals to attract funding for their research.

The research activities of TT faculty members result in publishing research articles, which are eventually cited and, over time, increase faculty members' *h-index*, that is, the number of articles cited at least *h* times. The combination of articles published, citations of these articles, and *h-index*, over time, provides an estimate of brand value, which correlates closely with an institution's rankings. This estimate is not a monetary value, but rather a composite performance indicator.

This is all complicated by several phenomena. Research funding is increasingly competitive, with funding decreasing relative to a steadily increasing number of proposals. Publication is increasingly competitive, with opportunities very constrained relative to a steadily increasing number of submissions. The result is faculty members have to work harder to achieve less success.

Revenue comes from tuition, research grants, and endowment earnings, as well as state budgets for public universities. Costs include those for teaching, research, administration, and overhead. Projections of revenues and costs yield model outputs that include various financial metrics, numbers of students and faculty, and brand value. University leaders have quickly found that cost versus reputation is a very central issue.

The tradeoff is very clear. Reducing percent TT lowers costs and, in principle at least, decreases tuition. Increasing percent TT increases costs and tuition but enhances brand value. Prospective students seek lower net tuition and higher brand value. Leaders of research universities have to decide where to position themselves relative to this tradeoff.

There are three scenarios of particular interest that may play out independently but have a combined effect on the results projected by the model:

- S1: Competition for federal dollars and publication in top journals is steadily increasing. The current success model at most research universities requires faculty members to work harder and harder to achieve less and less success, proposal writing consuming increasing time, and publication preparation receiving decreasing attention.
- S2: Foreign student enrollment in graduate programs has decreased in recent years due to competition from other countries and, more recently, concerns about US immigration policies. These professional master's degrees are typically "cash cows" for research universities, subsidizing many other aspects of the enterprise.
- S3: Highly polished, well-done online offerings will increasingly succeed. Once the credentials associated with success in these online courses are acceptable to employers, it is easy to imagine a massive shift away from traditional classrooms for some categories of students, especially those seeking professional credentials and master's degrees where distance learning is already recognized and increasingly common.

Using data from the Center for Measuring University Performance, the model was parameterized for four specific institutions – large vs. small and public vs. private – where size refers to resource availability, not the number of students.

SCENARIO PROJECTIONS

The three scenarios were more specifically defined as follows:

- S1: Status Quo
- S2: Graduate Student Population Declines by 5% Annually
- S3: Graduate Tuition Declines to $10,000 Due to Online Offerings

Note that class size was varied – to 10X or 1,000 – for the three instances of S3 rather than adding a fourth and fifth scenario, i.e., S3:$10K, S3:10X, and S3:1K.

S3:$10K is the worst scenario, resulting in negative net present value (NPV) of deficits for everyone because the number of students does not decrease while revenue decreases substantially. Three of the cases – S2, S3:10X, and S3:1K – lead to substantially reduced numbers of faculty, which undermines institutional publishing productivity and, hence, brand value. S3:1K is the most profitable because the number of students does not decrease but faculty numbers are cut by over 90%. Brand value, of course, plummets and makes all four institutions almost equivalent.

Institutions with resources are simply not going to let these futures happen to them. High-resource institutions have been the "first movers" in enabling S3:$10K. Thus, they are cannibalizing their professional master's "cash cows" before others do. They are likely to become the infrastructure platforms for others' educational content, although they may also be content providers to resource-poor institutions. This, of course, raises the possibility that these resource-poor institutions will disappear or be absorbed by others.

Overall, all these scenarios result in decreased research productivity due to diminishing returns for S1, and dramatically declining faculty sizes for S2 and S3. All four institutions that illustrate these scenarios benefit financially by decreasing subsidies for research, but the dramatic decrease in research output would certainly be a national concern. However, using student debt, at least in part, to subsidize research enterprises is not in the national interest. Some rethinking seems definitely warranted.

TECHNOLOGY INVESTMENTS

We imagine that different disciplines will address change in different ways, in part greatly dependent on the university resources available. We chose to address humanities, medicine, and engineering. However, we expect that schools of business and law will also face similar challenges. Nevertheless, the investments by discipline may differ significantly. Four types of investments seem likely.

Online Education

All disciplines will necessarily have to entertain greater use of online teaching, as the response to the pandemic has prompted. However, disciplines may differ in emphases. Some of these differences will be driven by the differing content employed in the curricula of these disciplines. Also of great importance will be the extent that face-to-face interactions are central to each discipline and the extent to which these interactions can be technologically mediated.

Interactive Technologies

Advanced technology can enable compelling interactive portrayals of phenomena ranging from chemistry and physics, to human physiology and behaviors, and to social and cultural interactions. These interactive technologies can augment reality and provide profound educational experiences. The quality of these immersive portrayals has steadily improved, and the costs, at least on widely available platforms, have progressively decreased. The economics of such technologies depend, however, on the number of students across which costs can be amortized.

Knowledge Management

Information access and knowledge management are challenges across disciplines, although the nature of data and knowledge artifacts differ substantially across disciplines. In particular, the technological infrastructure associated with science and technology has benefited from enormous investments. Humanities have seen important investments and innovations but not at all on the same scale. Of particular note, the data and knowledge artifacts of the humanities were seldom originally created digitally.

Process Improvement

Process modeling and improvement initiatives are significantly affected by two factors. One is the extent to which educational processes are interwoven with operational processes. This is greatest for medicine where much of the education happens during the delivery of clinical services. In engineering, considerable research happens with industry, and undergraduate cooperative education programs are pervasive. Humanities have few similar processes and thus can be approached in a more straightforward manner.

The second factor is scale. When an undergraduate major, e.g., electrical, industrial, or mechanical engineering, has well over 1,000 students in one department, technology investments can be amortized across many students and, thereby, justify much greater investments. If such institutions are also well resourced, the human and financial resources can be marshaled to undertake these investments.

Impacts on Ecosystem

We expect increased enrollments due to technology-enabled easier access and potentially lower-priced tuitions. With continuing pressures to control costs, there will be a steadily decreasing tenure track faculty workforce, with the possible exception of the strongest institutions.

Technology and outsourcing will result in steadily decreasing staff positions. Decreased investments in bricks and mortar will inevitably lead to fewer support staff. Overall university employment will decline, with possible exceptions in medicine where clinician deficits are projected, and possibly engineering with steadily increasing demands for science, technology, engineering, and math (STEM) education.

Impacts on Competitiveness

The overall result will be a better-educated workforce due to increased enrollments. There will be increased workforce diversity due to easier access and lower prices. This will lead to an increasingly healthy, educated, and productive workforce that is competitive in the global marketplace.

With faculty positions becoming scarcer, there will be the increased placement of PhD graduates in industry and government. This will lead to enhanced technology transfer and innovation due to broadened placement of research talent. Industry and government demand for professional graduate degrees will increase with easier access and lower prices.

STEM TALENT PIPELINE

More recently, we have undertaken a study of the STEM talent pipeline for DoD. They are concerned that the DoD workforce – both government and private sector – will not have sufficient US citizen STEM graduates for their workforce and the broader US technology workforce. As we have focused on finding the leverage points for increasing this workforce, we have encountered fundamental problems.

Sixteen percent of K–12 graduates in the USA are STEM-ready, meaning they have taken and passed courses in algebra I and II, geometry, trigonometry, pre-calculus, physics, chemistry, or biology. This low percentage is due in part to students not being motivated to take these difficult courses. However, an overarching limitation is many K–12 schools not offering these courses, not to mention the advanced placement offerings of these courses. Thus, a significant portion of US K–12 students could never become STEM-ready.

How could this happen? Public schools are funded by local property taxes and significant state funding, but relatively little federal funding. Keeping local and state taxes in check requires underfunding K–12. When I was growing up in a small New England town, we felt that we were all better off if everyone was educated. Now we feel that everyone is on their own to provide what they need in whatever way they can afford.

It is useful to reference these findings in *Perspectives on Complex Global Challenges* edited by Elisabeth Pate-Cornell, Charles Vest, and me. This edited collection of essays by a wide range of luminaries includes a section on education with contributions by university presidents and deans, and corporate chief executives. They articulate the need for transforming various aspects of higher education, as well as the K–12 talent pipeline feeding this system. This is a major national challenge.

CONCLUSIONS

The efforts in this chapter involved similar models, methods, and tools of previous chapters. However, my perspective changed substantially. First, we became less concerned with enterprise revenues and profits and more focused on effective and affordable social services. Second, our purview moved from individual enterprises to broader public–private enterprises. Consequently, behavioral and social phenomena became increasingly prevalent.

My purview will become even broader in Chapter 10 on societal systems. First, however, Chapter 9 integrates our models, methods, and tools into an overall methodology. This integration sets the stage for their application to understanding complex global challenges and contributing to addressing them.

EPILOGUE

I moved from Hoboken to Washington in late December 2016, staying in a hotel for a couple of weeks until my lease at Cathedral Commons near the Washington National Cathedral commenced. I had pretty much completed my New York City bucket list, which included many museums, Central Park, Fifth Avenue window shopping, a Broadway show, Greenwich Village, Strand Bookstore, Eataly, 9/11 Memorial, Rockefeller Center, Circle Line cruise around Manhattan, Coney Island, and Montauk Point.

I knew I would miss New York pizza and the rich happy hour routine of Hoboken. I have not missed the airports, perilous traffic (for pedestrians), overall dirtiness and litter, and New Yorkers' general impatience with everything. In a way, I feel that I was "stationed" in New York City, served my time, gained invaluable knowledge and experience, and moved to a place where it is much easier to relax. More on this later.

My office at Stevens was on the fifth floor of Babbio Center, with a panoramic view of Manhattan. Across the Hudson to the right was the former site of the Fall River Line piers where my great great-grandfather's passenger ships docked. I discovered and purchased an 1894 print of his ship Priscilla – the Queen of Long Island Sound – leaving the dock on the way to Boston.

This connection caused me to research the history of greater New York City. I started with John Jacob Astor in the 18th century and chronicled the contributions of 40 innovators up until Michael Bloomberg in the 21st century. These contributions ranged from aviation to automobiles, banking to finance, communications to computing, electricity to oil, and railroads to retail and fashion. These findings are presented in *A Century of Innovation.*

This material provided the basis for a lecture I gave at the New York Yacht Club on "How Greater New York City Transformed America." I gave the talk in the Model Room, which hosts the yacht models of many famous members of the Club. Many of the models belonged to the famous innovators I highlighted in my lecture. It was quite a compelling experience with many top executives and media folks in the audience.

I gave this lecture several times at other venues. One was to insurance industry executives at Chart House in Weehawken on the Hudson River as evening arrived and Manhattan was ablaze with lights. It was another perfect backdrop for this story. I think these experiences were uniquely New York and gave me a very rich sense of the city and its people.

FURTHER READING

Rouse, W.B. (2014). *A Century of Innovation: From Wooden Sailing Ships to Electric Railways, Computers, Space Travel and Internet.* Raleigh: Lulu Press.

Rouse, W.B. (2015). *Modeling and Visualization of Complex Systems and Enterprises: Explorations of Physical, Human, Economic, and Social Phenomena.* Hoboken: John Wiley & Sons.

Rouse, W.B. (2016). *Universities as Complex Enterprises: How Academia Works, Why It Works These Ways, and Where the University Enterprise Is Headed.* Hoboken: John Wiley & Sons.

Rouse, W.B., & Cortese, D.A. (Eds.).(2010). *Engineering the System of Healthcare Delivery.* Amsterdam: IOS Press.

Rouse, W.B., & Serban, N. (2014). *Understanding and Managing the Complexity of Healthcare.* Cambridge: MIT Press.

9

Modeling and Visualization

PROLOGUE

Once you have perfected a few recipes, there is a seemingly natural tendency to formulate a cookbook to enable others to match your successes. In the earlier chapters of this book, I have presented and illustrated a range of concepts, principles, models, methods, and tools. You have read the equivalent of treatises on hammers, saws, screwdrivers, and wrenches.

In this chapter, I discuss a set of ten steps that form a methodology for applying all these tools to achieve success in addressing almost any problem or question. The ambitions to develop such a methodology are rife with risks. Why do the nature and order of the proposed steps make sense? What are the other possibilities? What is the evidence that the methodology has worked in the past and will work in the future?

These questions challenge the uniqueness of a methodology in terms of its utility and usability for addressing problems of interest. Is it *the* methodology or *a* methodology for achieving success? Agreeing to the latter does not mean that *any* methodology will suffice. There are many approaches that are simply bad ideas. We want to avoid these while refining and extending approaches that work. From this perspective, the methodology I discuss in this chapter is a work in progress.

INTRODUCTION

A methodology is a set of steps for accomplishing something, in our case, designing and evaluating products, services, or policies. The steps

DOI: 10.4324/9781003365549-9

are usually formulated to make sure the types of things associated with success are accomplished. In others words, the right issues are addressed and resolved.

A methodology can also help to avoid missteps. That is a central concern here. The methodology described in this chapter is intended to avoid incorrect formulation of problems. Engineering is often taught as a set of models and techniques such as theories of dynamic systems, networks, process flows, decision making, and so forth.

This approach to packaging knowledge often leads engineers to automatically classify problems as system dynamics, discrete event flows, or agent decision making. Once classified in this way, it can be difficult to get them to consider alternative representations. They have already decided the nature of the problem. However, they are only actually working on their representation of the problem.

A further difficulty is that they have, in effect, already decided the nature of the solution. They have decided the solution is a matter of controlling system state, process flows, etc. Succinctly, they have jumped to a solution, motivated by their abilities to execute this solution. This is a proverbial problem of someone who only has a hammer – everything looks like a nail!

In this chapter, I outline the modeling and visualization methodology used to conduct many of the endeavors discussed in earlier chapters. This methodology is intended to avoid these natural inclinations. I weave five themes into this discussion.

- Understanding the essential phenomena underlying the overall behaviors of complex systems can enable improving these systems.
- These phenomena range from physical, behavioral, and organizational to economic and social, all of which involve significant human components.
- Specific phenomena of interest and how they are represented depend on the questions of interest and the relevant domains or contexts.
- Visualization of phenomena and relationships among phenomena can provide the basis for understanding where deeper exploration is warranted.
- Mathematical and computational models, defined *very* broadly across disciplines, can enable the necessary deeper understanding.

PHENOMENA

The construct of "phenomena" is central to this chapter. Problem solving should not begin with the selection of mathematical or computational models but instead should commence with consideration of the phenomena that must be understood to successfully answer the questions that motivated the modeling effort in the first place. Typically, these phenomena underlie the nature of the question of interest.

Definitions

What is meant by the term "phenomena"? There are many definitions that depend on the context of use – for example, a particular jazz saxophonist might be characterized as a "phenomenon." Within the context of science and engineering, examples include elasticity, specific weight, viscosity, specific heat content, melting point, electrical resistance, thermal conductivity, magnetic permeability, physical hysteresis, crystallinity, refractivity, chemical affinity, wavelength, chemical diffusivity, solubility, electric field strength, superconductivity, and atomic force. These examples fit into the framework elaborated in this chapter but form only a small part of the spectrum of phenomena of interest in this book.

Science seeks to discover and understand the nature of phenomena, particularly at a scale or in a world not open to direct human observation. Technologists use science because it is the only way to understand how phenomena work at deeper or broader layers. Science is the probing of phenomena via technology.

Inventors learned how to harness, control, and design phenomena ranging from steam to electricity, and from internal combustion to aerodynamic lift to analog and digital computation. Innovators found ways to bring these controlled phenomena to the marketplace to provide value to people.

How does technology transfer to market innovation? This has been a question of great interest for several decades. James Burke reaches two all-embracing conclusions. First, the application originally envisioned for new technology is hardly ever the application on which the technology has its greatest impact. Second, the original investor in a new technology is hardly ever the recipient of the greatest returns enabled by the technology. Interest in the management of innovation has been motivated by desires to avoid this destiny.

Succinctly, technology involves harnessing phenomena to purposeful ends. Often, phenomena are first characterized and then understood by science. Engineering, and inventors, in particular, determines how to harness the phenomena, often long before scientists have determined how best to characterize the phenomena. Innovation results when the value proposition for delivering the benefits of the phenomena makes sense in a marketplace. Eventually, this value proposition is disrupted, new technologies displace the old, and creative destruction moves the economy and society forward.

Historical Perspectives

The history of harnessing phenomena to purposeful ends is rich with examples of ingenuity and determination. In some cases, it took hundreds and even thousands of years from recognition and understanding of a phenomenon to fully leveraging it for useful ends.

Steam to Steamboats

Greek philosophers argued that the four fundamental natural phenomena were earth, air, fire, and water. Much was accomplished with these phenomena. Water and fire were combined to yield steam. By the first century AD, people had discovered that water heated in a closed vessel produced high-pressure steam that could be used to power various novelty devices. Channeling the pressure using a cylinder led to Thomas Newcomen's steam engine in 1712. James Watt added an external condenser in 1776 so that condensation did not result in significant losses of heat. Robert Fulton used Watt's engine and a hull designed for this mode of propulsion to develop the first commercially successful steamboat, the Clermont, in 1807. Thus, steam to steamboats took roughly 1,800 years.

Wind to Wings

Air in the form of wind is a phenomenon that was exploited quite early. Wind plus cloth sails led to sailboats by 4000 BC. Wind plus vanes (frameworks for sails) plus wooden gears led to windmills by 1000 AD. Wind plus lift plus thrust led to heavier than air flight in 1800–1900. Thrust is needed to create movement, and hence wind, to enable the lifting phenomena of airfoils. Thus, powered flight emerged in 1903. Wind to wings took almost 5,000 years.

Electricity to Lights

Electricity was not one of the original four fundamental phenomena. However, static electricity was known by 600 BC. Magnetism was known then as well, but it was not until 1600 that William Gilbert outlined the relationship between electricity and magnetism, which James Clerk Maxwell formalized in 1873. Earlier, in 1752, Benjamin Franklin combined lightning, a wetted kite string, and a key to demonstrate the phenomenon of electricity. By 1802, Humphrey Davy had shown that electricity when passed through platinum produced light. Warren de la Rue enclosed a coiled platinum filament in a vacuum tube and passed an electric current through it in 1840 for the first light bulb.

In 1878, Thomas Edison created a light bulb with a more effective incandescent material, a better vacuum, and high resistance that also made power distribution from a centralized source economically viable. His Pearl Street Station in New York City meant that houses in that area only had to install electric lights. They did not have to produce their own electricity. This made the adoption of his innovation much easier. The path from knowledge of electricity to viable electric lighting systems took almost 2,500 years. In all three of these examples, harnessing known phenomena to useful ends took many centuries.

Macro and Micro Physics

Other phenomena of historical interest include the inventions of Leonardo Da Vinci (1452–1519), harnessing motion, force, and flow for his civil and military work. Isaac Newton (1643–1727) studied the motions of planets and created calculus in the process, although Gottfried Leibniz (1643–1716) claimed credit for calculus as well. Albert Einstein (1879–1955) articulated a special theory of relativity in 1905 and a general theory in 1916, thereby relegating Newton's theory of mechanics to the status of a special case for objects whose movements are much slower than the speed of light. Special relativity concerns interactions of elementary particles, while general relativity applies to phenomena of cosmology and astrophysics.

Behaviors of elementary particles became phenomena of much scientific interest as the 19th century gave way to the 20th. Joseph Thomson (1856–1940) discovered the electron in 1897. Ernest Rutherford (1871–1937) discovered the nucleus in 1909. Niels Bohr (1885–1962) added the notion of fixed orbits of the electron in 1913. Louis de Broglie (1892–1987) contributed to the wave theory of subatomic particles in 1924, which was extended by Erwin Schrödinger (1887–1961) in 1926. The inherent uncertainties associated with wave behaviors led Werner Heisenberg (1901–76) to articulate his uncertainty principle in 1927.

Four Fundamental Forces

Thoughts about fundamental phenomena have come a long way since earth, air, fire, and water had this honor. Contemporary physicists and other scientists see fundamental nature as involving four constructs – gravitation, electromagnetism, strong nuclear force, and weak nuclear force. Gravitation and electromagnetism are the only two we experience in everyday life. The strong and weak nuclear forces operate at distances of femtometers (10^{-15} meters) or less.

Gravitation affects macroscopic objects over macroscopic distances. It is the only force that acts on all particles having mass and has an infinite range. Gravity cannot be absorbed, transformed, or shielded against. Gravity always attracts; it never repels.

Electromagnetism is the force that acts between electrically charged particles. This phenomenon includes the electrostatic force acting between charged particles at rest, as well as the effects of electric and magnetic forces acting between charged particles as they move relative to each other.

The strong and weak nuclear forces pertain to phenomena within the atomic nucleus. The strong force varies with distance and is practically unobservable at distances greater than 10^{-15} meters. The weak nuclear force is responsible for some nuclear phenomena such as beta decay.

This notion that these four fundamental phenomena underlie everything does not seem as compelling as earth, air, fire, and water, at least from an engineering perspective. Yet, understanding, predicting, and then controlling these forces may, in some distant future, lead to amazing innovations and subsequent innovations.

FRAMEWORK

This brief tour of the history of physical phenomena is a starting point for consideration of the full range of phenomena relevant to problems that I discuss throughout this book. We developed a framework for thinking about phenomena and relationships among phenomena. There are four levels – physical, human, economic, and social – as well as typical relationships among phenomena. We typically addressed eight classes of phenomena, occurring across multiple levels of an ecosystem, as shown in Figure 9.1:

- Physical, natural: temporal and spatial relationships and responses.
- Physical, designed: input–output relationships, responses, stability.
- Human, individuals: task behaviors and performance, mental models.
- Human, teams, or groups: team and group behavior and performance.
- Economic, micro: consumer value, pricing, production economics.
- Economic, macro: gross production, employment, inflation, taxation.
- Social, organizational: structures, roles, information, resources.
- Social, societal: castes, constituencies, coalitions, negotiations.

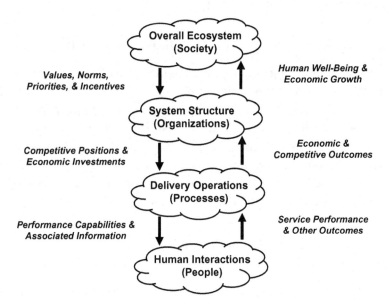

FIGURE 9.1
Multi-level Framework.

I discuss and illustrate the nature of these classes of phenomena in depth in *Modeling and Visualization of Complex Systems and Enterprises*. Of particular note, the first two classes represent phenomena underlying the physics of problems. The other six classes are often associated with why problems are problems. They encompass the behavioral and social phenomena that underlie the motivations to understand and remediate performance shortfalls in terms of outcomes and costs of these outcomes. In general, we understand physical phenomena better than the other classes, but we are rapidly accumulating an understanding of these classes as well.

METHODOLOGY

Experience has shown that models should be developed with a clear intent, with defined scope and givens. Initial emphasis should be on alternative views of phenomena important to addressing the questions of interest. Selected views can then be more formally modeled and simulated. I have found that the following ten-step methodology provides a structure to support this approach to modeling.

Step 1: Decide on the Central Questions of Interest

The history of modeling and simulation is littered with failures of attempts to develop models without clear intentions in mind. Models provide means to answer questions. Efforts to model socio-technical systems are often motivated by decision makers' questions about the feasibility and efficacy of decisions on policy, strategy, operations, etc. The first step is to discuss the questions of interest with the decision maker(s) and other stakeholders, define what they need to know to feel that the questions are answered, and agree on key variables of interest.

Step 2: Define Key Phenomena Underlying These Questions

The next step involves defining the key phenomena that underlie the variables associated with the questions of interest. Phenomena can range from physical, behavioral, or organizational to economic, social, or political. Broad classes of phenomena across these domains include continuous and discrete flows, manual and automatic control, resource allocation, and individual and collective choice. Mature domains have often developed standard descriptions of relevant phenomena.

Step 3: Develop One or More Visualizations of Relationships among Phenomena

Phenomena can often be described in terms of inputs, processes, and outputs. Often the inputs of one phenomenon are the outputs of other phenomena. Common variables among phenomena provide a basis for visualization of the set of key phenomena. Common visualization methods include block diagrams, integrated definition methods, influence diagrams, and systemigrams.

Step 4: Determine Key Tradeoffs That Appear to Warrant Deeper Exploration

The visualizations resulting from Step 3 often provide the basis for in-depth discussions and debates among members of the modeling team as well as the sponsors of the effort, which hopefully includes the decision makers who intend to use the results of the modeling effort to inform their decisions, as well as stakeholders in these decisions. Lines of reasoning, perhaps only qualitative, are often verbalized that provide the means for immediate resolution of some issues, as well as dismissal of some issues that no longer seem to matter. New issues may, of course, also arise.

Step 5: Identify Alternative Representations of These Phenomena

Computational representations are needed for those phenomena that will be explored in more depth. These representations include equations, curves, surfaces, process models, agent models, etc. – in general, instantiations of standard representations. Boundary conditions can affect choices of representations. This requires deciding on fixed and variable boundary conditions such as GDP growth, inflation, carbon emissions, etc. Fixed conditions can be embedded in representations, while variable conditions require controls such as slider bars to accommodate variations – see Step 9.

Step 6: Assess the Ability to Connect Alternative Representations

Representations of phenomena associated with tradeoffs to be addressed in more depth usually require inputs from other representations and produce outputs required by yet other representations. Representations may differ in terms of dichotomies such as linear vs. nonlinear, static vs. dynamic, deterministic vs. stochastic, continuous vs. discrete, and so on. They may also differ in terms of basic assumptions, e.g., Markov vs. non-Markovian processes. This step involves determining what can be meaningfully connected together. There are major opportunities for missteps when representations are inherently incompatible. Plugging them together may lead to erroneous predictions.

Step 7: Determine a Consistent Set of Assumptions

The set of assumptions associated with the representations that are to be computationally connected need to be consistent for the results of these computations to be meaningful. At the very least, this involves synchronizing time across representations, standardizing variable definitions and units of measures, and agreeing on a common coordinate system or appropriate transformations among differing coordinate systems. It also involves dealing consistently with continuity, conservation, and independence assumptions.

Step 8: Identify Data Sets to Support Parameterization

The set of representations chosen and refined in Steps 5–7 will have parameters such as transition probabilities, time constants, and decay rates that have to be estimated using data from the domain(s) in which the questions of interest are to be addressed. Data sources need to be identified, and the conditions under which these data were collected determined. Estimation methods need to be chosen, and in some cases, developed, to provide unbiased estimates of model parameters.

Step 9: Program and Verify Computational Instantiations

To the extent possible, this step is best accomplished with commercially available software tools. The prototyping and debugging capabilities of such tools are often well worth the price. A variant of this proposal is to use commercial tools to prototype and refine the overall model. Once the design of the model is fixed, one can then develop custom software for production runs. The versions in the commercial tools can then be used to verify the custom code. This step also involves instantiating interactive visualizations with graphs, charts, sliders, radio buttons, etc.

Step 10: Validate Model Predictions, at Least Against Baseline Data

The last step involves validating the resulting model. This can be difficult when the model has been designed to explore policies, strategies, etc., for which there are inherently no empirical data. A weak form of validation is possible by using the model to predict current performance with the "as is" policies, strategies, etc. In general, models used to explore "what if" possibilities are best employed to gain insights that can be used to frame propositions for subsequent empirical study.

The logic of the ten-step methodology can be summarized as follows, with emphasis on Steps 1–7:

- Define the question(s) of interest.
- Identify relevant phenomena.
- Visually compose phenomena.
- Identify useful representations.
- Computationally compose representations.

Note that this logic places great emphasis on problem framing and formulation. Deep computation is preserved for visually identified critical tradeoffs rather than the whole problem formulation. Steps 8–10 of the methodology are common to many methodologies.

Not all problems require full use of this ten-step methodology. Often visual portrayals of phenomena and relationships are sufficient to provide insights of interest. For example, I have often encountered problems where simple visualizations of the problem enabled decision makers to immediately understand what needed to be done. As just noted, such views are also valuable for determining which aspects of the problem should be explored more deeply.

VISUALIZATION

Thus, not all problems or questions require deep computational exploration. Visual portrayals of phenomena can lead to almost immediate recognition of where a mechanism might fail, or a process flow will lead to bottlenecks, or an incentive system may prompt unintended consequences. In particular, visualization of phenomena can assist in identifying the portions of the overall problem that may merit deep computational modeling. This is central to Step 4 of the overall methodology.

Purposes

Beyond being aesthetically appealing, visualizations are usually intended to serve some useful purpose. Indeed, without purposes, visualizations are all just colors and curves. Not surprisingly, it is important to define the purpose of the visualization before, or at least during, its creation.

- Visualization enables digesting huge amounts of data.
- Visualization enables the perception of emergent properties.
- Visualization enables data problems to become immediately apparent.
- Visualization enables understanding of multiple scales of data.
- Visualization enables formation of hypotheses.

Jens Rasmussen, a colleague I mentioned earlier, addressed the role of visualizations in operating and maintaining complex engineered systems such as nuclear power plants. He argued for the merits of thinking about information displays in terms of abstraction and aggregation. He proposed the following abstraction hierarchy:

- Functional Purpose – production flow models, system objectives.
- Abstract Function – causal structure; mass, energy, and information flow topology.
- Generalized Functions – standard functions, processes, control loops, heat transfer.
- Physical Functions – electrical, mechanical, chemical processes of equipment.

- Physical Form – physical appearance and anatomy, material and form, locations, etc.

Thus, the purpose of a system is a more abstract concept than how it functions. In turn, the systems' abstract and generalized functions are more abstract than their physical functions and forms.

Levels of aggregation are best illustrated in terms of the decomposition of a system, for example, an automobile. At the abstraction level of physical form, the vehicle can be decomposed into power train, suspension, frame, etc. The power train can be decomposed into engine, transmission, drive shaft, differentials, and wheels. The engine can be decomposed into blocks and cylinders, pistons, camshaft, valves, etc. As noted, these levels of aggregation are all represented within the same level of abstraction – physical form.

Rasmussen's hierarchies of abstraction and aggregation play a central role in the visualization design methodology that I outline below. One can view a use case in terms of a set of visualizations as a trajectory in an abstraction–aggregation space. Each point in this space will have one or more associated visualizations. Each of these visualizations may portray, individually or in combination, data (e.g., performance history of subsystems), structure (e.g., what connects to what), dynamics (e.g., response over time), or other pertinent representations.

Step 1: Identify Information Use Cases, Including Knowledge Levels of Users

Use cases provide descriptions of alternative ways in which users will employ the visualizations to achieve their purposes – *before* the visualizations have been created. These high-level descriptions can be characterized in terms of six general tasks:

- *Retrieve* data and visualizations relevant to questions of interest.
- *Recognize* characteristics of interest across chosen attributes.
- *Construct* or select and parameterize representations provided.
- *Compute* outputs of constructed representations over time.
- *Compare* outputs to objectives or across output variations.
- *Refine* constructed representations and return to *Compute*.

Step 2: Define Trajectories in Abstraction–Aggregation Space

Use cases define what information is needed and what actions are taken at every step of the task of interest. This includes the levels of abstraction and aggregation for requisite information elements and controls for each task.

Step 3: Design Visualizations and Controls for Each Point in Space

Transform the outputs of Step 2 into what, specifically, users can see and do. There is a wealth of possibilities, which need to be compiled into a manageable set of choices. Note that many of the possibilities will be domain dependent.

Step 4: Integrate across Visualizations and Controls to Dovetail Representations

Visualizations and controls should not completely change for each step in a task. Integrated visualizations may be able to support more than one step. Individual controls may affect more than one view.

Step 5: Integrate across Use Cases to Minimize the Total Number of Displays and Controls

The set of visualizations may serve more than one purpose. For example, novices may use it to learn about a domain, while experts use it to address real problems of interest. Experts may, for example, see the same central visualizations as novices but have access to additional information and controls to enable manipulations of phenomena that novices would not understand.

Immersion Lab

The visualization elements can be integrated to create an overall interactive visualization. The issue of how best to integrate these various elements quickly arises when addressing questions of interest in the context of a complex system in a particular domain. Consideration of this issue led to the notion of an *Immersion Lab* and the following observations:

- Many of the phenomena in our critical public–private systems are very complex and becoming more so.
- Many of the key stakeholders in these systems are not technically sophisticated, yet they have an enormous influence on outcomes.
- These stakeholders can be engaged and influenced by being immersed in the complexity of their domain.
- The *Immersion Lab* can attract key stakeholders and sponsors to interactive problem-solving and decision-making sessions.
- If the interactive visualizations are well conceived and integrated, many people will report that they did not realize what they experienced was possible.

Our version of an *Immersion Lab* included an 8-foot by 20-foot, 180-degree visualization platform with seven touch-sensitive displays. These large touch displays could be driven in any combination, ranging from seven independent displays to one large, integrated display. Local display generation computers, linked to nearby supercomputer capabilities, drove the displays.

The *Immersion Lab* was used frequently in two modes. One was the development and use of particular models such as the New York City health ecosystem discussed in Chapter 8 and the automotive marketplace discussed in Chapter 10. The other use was by industry executive teams to explore a variety of phenomena of interest to them in their marketplace. In this way, they immersed themselves in a variety of portrayals of these phenomena.

The point is that the interactive visualizations were key to engaging important stakeholders in the process of understanding underlying phenomena, exploring relationships among phenomena, and discussing and debating a wide range of "what if" questions. A canned PowerPoint presentation cannot possibly enable such rich interchanges and stakeholder buy-in.

CONCLUSIONS

The concepts and methods I have discussed in this chapter provide a template that has been employed for many of the endeavors outlined in earlier chapters. However, we never used this template in a lock-step fashion. Instead, it provided guidance on what to do next if there was not a compelling argument to do otherwise. It also served as a checklist to assure important things were not missed. It helped us to avoid jumping to solutions.

The central element of this methodology is the great emphasis on problem formulation prior to contemplating a problem solution. Unfortunately, the culture of engineering is solution oriented. However, complex problems laced with behavioral and social phenomena are often not amenable to quick solutions. Often, much more negotiation is needed, as Steps 1–3 of the methodology emphasize. This can frustrate solution-driven members of the team. I have found that advance agreement on the conduct of the methodology can ameliorate these frustrations as everyone realizes the sequence of steps that will be pursued.

One particular facilitation technique can help. Namely, when one or more team members feel that they know the solution needed, this solution can be captured in a "parking lot" of ideas to be revisited later in the process. Solution-oriented team members often feel reassured that their ideas are waiting in the wings for later evaluation, often on a flip chart that they and everyone else can see. Process-oriented team members seldom object to this. Keep in mind that the overall process has to work for both team members and other stakeholders.

EPILOGUE

So, does the methodology work? My colleagues Mike Pennock and Doug Bodner conducted a couple of studies to evaluate this methodology. I think it is fair to say that they concluded the methodology is fine in general but likely needs some modification for particular problems. This conclusion is fine with me. The methodology provides guidelines, not a catechism.

I do not think a methodology can be proven "correct." It can only be shown to be usable and useful – or not. Of course, as noted earlier, a methodology can be outright wrong. However, these bad ideas are seldom the benchmarks against which new ideas are compared. I am perfectly happy to have *one* of the good ideas.

I find the notion of phenomena increasingly compelling. Formulating a problem should start with understanding and portraying the physical, human, economic, and social phenomena underlying the problem. This exploration should be more like cultural anthropology than mathematical physics. It involves observing and listening to stakeholders and representing what you learn, often in sketches and diagrams. You are looking for understanding rather than answers.

The methodology I have presented in this chapter starts by leveraging what you have learned into an overall formulation of the problem of interest. Alternative problem solutions come later, as indicated in the methodology. It requires discipline to avoid jumping to solutions. All too often, such jumps are unproductive, resulting in wasted time and resources. If you think you know the answer immediately, you are probably wrong.

It can be valuable to capture solution ideas proposed along the way, perhaps in the Parking Lot. In keeping with set-based design, there is no need to home in on *the* solution. A portfolio of possible solutions can be invaluable. These may be of value for helping to address other problems later. If you are good at solving the problem at hand, you will likely be called upon for future problems. Thus, notes and observations on what was not pursued can be quite useful.

FURTHER READING

Rouse, W.B. (2015). *Modeling And Visualization of Complex Systems and Enterprises: Explorations of Physical, Human, Economic, And Social Phenomena*. New York: Wiley.

Rouse, W.B. (2019). *Computing Possible Futures: Model Based Explorations of "What If?"* Oxford, UK: Oxford University Press.

Rouse, W.B. (2021). *Failure Management: Malfunctions of Technologies, Organizations, and Society*. Oxford, UK: Oxford University Press.

Sage, A.P., & Rouse, W.B. (2011). *Economic System Analysis and Assessment*. New York: Wiley.

10

Complex Societal Systems

PROLOGUE

My move to Washington, DC, immersed me in a very different ecosystem than New York City or Atlanta – or Boston, for that matter. This small city of 70 square miles and 700,000 residents is at the center of the National Capitol Region – or DMV for DC, Maryland, and Virginia – with a total population of over 6 million people occupying 5,500 square miles.

DC has the highest average education level in the USA as well as the highest per capita income. It is home to the three branches of the federal government, the main embassies of every country represented in the USA, and a wealth of museums and monuments. Half of the think tanks in the USA are based in DC. Professional sports teams have, of late, done fairly well with the Capitals, Mystics, and Nationals having recently won titles.

Unfortunately, DC also has one of the highest poverty levels in the USA. DC is 45% black, 43% white, and 4% Asian. Wards 7 and 8 are predominantly black, but blacks account for only 5% of the population in Ward 3 where I live – Cathedral Heights. Thus, the education levels and affluence of DC are far from evenly distributed. This is obviously a major challenge for the city.

I have not owned a car in DC. The Metro and bus system are pervasive and inexpensive, occasionally abetted by Uber when time is tight. People 65 or over, like me, can travel anyplace in the city by bus for one dollar. Public transit is clean, unlike in New York City, and passengers are polite and friendly. I do not often sense people being stressed out by the transit system.

DC is also a very walkable city, with wide streets and ample sidewalks. I live close to the National Zoo. My walk to the Zoo takes me through neighborhoods of large Victorian homes with beautiful landscaping. There are also ample green spaces, most public but many privately owned and open to the public. DC is a place very much of neighborhoods, with people knowing each other and stopping to chat.

I have found the intellectual diversity of people in DC to be very interesting. The person sitting next to you at the bar may work in a government agency, an embassy, a non-profit, or a major technology company. I have yet to encounter anyone working for a hedge fund. Email addresses are often exchanged. You never know where the connections will lead.

INTRODUCTION

The move to DC was motivated by more than just the attractiveness of the city. Most of my research sponsors and many colleagues are based here. Easy access to the National Academies, where I have been active for 40 years and an elected member for over 30 years, provides numerous opportunities to become immersed in societal issues and challenges. More broadly, there is talent everywhere. DC is a very opportunity-rich environment.

There are abundant opportunities to address complexity. Systems can be simple, complicated, complex, or chaotic as outlined by the contributors to *Complex Socio-Technical Systems*. These authors wrestled with the nature of causality in complex systems. For the types of systems of interest here, causality is not as simple as Newton's apple, although the philosophers at the workshop convincingly argued that the apple is not really all that simple.

COMPLEX ADAPTIVE SYSTEMS

The nature of human and social phenomena within the systems discussed in this chapter is a central consideration. Systems where such phenomena play substantial roles are often considered to belong to a class of systems termed complex adaptive systems. Systems of this type have the following characteristics:

- They tend to be *nonlinear and dynamic* and do not inherently reach fixed equilibrium points. The resulting system behaviors may appear to be random or chaotic.

- They are composed of *independent agents* whose behaviors can be described as based on physical, psychological, or social rules, rather than being completely dictated by the physical dynamics of the system.
- Agents' needs or desires, reflected in their rules, are not homogeneous, and, therefore, their *goals and behaviors are likely to differ or even conflict* – these conflicts or competitions tend to lead agents to adapt to each other's behaviors.
- Agents are *intelligent and learn* as they experiment and gain experience, perhaps via "meta" rules, and consequently change behaviors. Thus, overall system properties inherently change over time.
- Adaptation and learning tend to result in *self-organization* and patterns of behavior that emerge rather than being designed into the system. The nature of such emergent behaviors may range from valuable innovations to unfortunate accidents.
- There are *no single point(s) of control* – system behaviors are often unpredictable and uncontrollable, and no one is "in charge." Consequently, the behaviors of complex adaptive systems usually can be influenced more than they can be controlled.

As might be expected, understanding and influencing systems having these characteristics creates significant complications. For example, the use of simulations to represent such systems often does not yield the same results each time they are run. Random variation may lead to varying "tipping points" among stakeholders for different simulation runs. Simulation models can be useful in the exploration of leading indicators of the different tipping points and in assessing potential mitigations for undesirable outcomes.

UNDERLYING PHENOMENA

There are a variety of challenges in addressing complex adaptive systems. The first challenge is to understand the central phenomena that underlie an ecosystem. What are the "physics" of the ecosystem and the rules of the game? Subject matter experts are usually essential to make sure central phenomena are considered and understood.

Second, one needs to understand the stakeholders associated with each of these phenomena. Who are the economic, technical, and user influences? Are there social and political influences? How are influences empowered and resourced? What are their values, concerns, and perceptions?

Third, one needs to understand how to impact the central phenomena. Typically, impacts are through stakeholders or agents. One needs to also understand stakeholders' likely responses to your attempts to impact them. You need to understand how to cultivate positive responses to your initiatives.

WICKED PROBLEMS

Problems associated with a complex adaptive ecosystem often easily qualify as "wicked problems." Horst Rittel, almost five decades ago, characterized wicked problems as social or cultural problems laced with incomplete or contradictory knowledge, large numbers of people and opinions involved, substantial economic burdens, and the interconnected nature of these problems with other problems. Problems such as poverty, sustainability, equality, health and wellness, and climate change are wicked problems that challenge our nation and our world.

Consider Rittel's ten characteristics of wicked problems. Wicked problems have no definitive formulation, i.e., they are not exemplars of any standard taxonomy of problems. It is difficult to measure or claim success in solving wicked problems, in part, because solutions can be only better or worse, but not correct or incorrect.

Given the uniqueness of each wicked problem, there are few, if any, best practices that can be adopted from the previous problem solving. This is due, in part, to every problem being a symptom of other problems. This is aggravated by there always being multiple explanations for problems, especially when there are many stakeholders.

Solutions to problems involve a single chance of success because one is trying to address a moving target driven by the complex adaptive nature of the ecosystem. Consequently, solution strategies have no definitive validity tests. Dealing with such situations requires that policy decision makers be empowered and responsible, keeping in mind that rarely is there one decision authority.

OVERALL APPROACH

In this section, I provide several qualitative guidelines for addressing complex adaptive organizational ecosystems. It should not be surprising that these guidelines are laced with principles from human-centered design.

Characterize the Nature of the Wicked Problem

What makes the problem at hand wicked? Are there large numbers of different types of stakeholders? Are there inherent conflicts among stakeholder groups? Are there reasons to expect any groups will try to stymie or undermine solutions to the problem? In general, it is important to be very honest and clear about likely difficulties.

Identify Anticipated or Experienced Value Deficiencies

What are the value deficiencies and how are they manifested? Typical examples include performance that is poor, slow, and expensive. Diminished competitive advantage is another, perhaps due to under-investment in new capabilities. Determine whether deficiencies are widely recognized or known only to a few people.

Determine What Processes Need to Be Resigned or Designed

What organizational processes underlie the value deficiencies? How are these processes contributing to the value deficiencies? Do these processes need to be substantially improved or completely replaced? Identify the stakeholders most aligned with sustaining the status quo.

Engage Stakeholders in How They Would Proceed with Changes

It is essential to involve those stakeholders who will be central to enabling and living with any changes. Seek their insights into the sources of value deficiencies. Solicit their ideas for redesigns or new designs. Make sure that a representative subset of these people is on the team.

Synthesize an Integrated Approach Across Contexts and Time

Consider how alternative solutions will dovetail with contexts, e.g., finance, personnel, and operations. Develop staged plans to implement changes over time. Be realistic about the number of stages and time likely needed. Make sure that the whole team understands the staging and timing.

Involve Stakeholders to Support These Changes, Likely Incrementally

Carefully manage stakeholders' expectations of the current stage of implementation so that they do not see this as overwhelming. Inform them that the downstream stages of implementation will be reconsidered and adapted as necessary once the current stage is done.

Secure and Sustain Resources to Accomplish Changes

Make sure that human and financial resources are sufficiently budgeted to be successful. Insufficient budgets will diminish the likelihood of success. Lack of success will undermine stakeholder support. This can easily change the cultural mood from optimism to pessimism and perhaps cynicism.

Execute Changes, Learning along the Way, and Adapting

Execute plans, keeping an eye on lessons learned about hindrances, i.e., things more difficult than expected, and affordances, i.e., things easier than expected. Solicit comments and suggestions on the compilation of lessons learned, including implications for the next stage. Be on the lookout for people with leadership proclivities and leverage their talents for subsequent stages.

Layered across these eight guidelines are three action principles:

- Think long term but act short term, creating relatively quick wins.
- Leverage support of quick wins to enable planning for the next wins.
- Learn from early wins to rethink plans for the next wins.

Possible quick wins to address include diminishing emphases on compliance, increasing reliance on technologies, increasing high-quality services, and incentivizing the adoption of new approaches. Any of these may be happening already and can be leveraged, as well as enhanced.

The case studies discussed in the remainder of this chapter differ from those in earlier chapters in the breadth of scope and the extent to which properties of complex adaptive systems are manifested and need to be addressed.

HEALTH

In this section, I consider three complex societal problems – cancer control, the opioid abuse epidemic, and the coronavirus pandemic. All three of these problems pose complex challenges for society. Recognition of this complexity and systematically addressing it are, I argue, key to managing these challenges.

Cancer Control

Michael Johns, former CEO of Emory Health and Michigan Health, and I had been collaborating for over ten years on prevention, wellness, and population health. We had been trying to convince the National Academy of Engineering and the National Academy of Medicine to consider the whole health and wellness system, not just medical practices. This would include consideration of education and social services to address, for example, social determinants of health.

We were slowly making progress, impeded in part by the simple fact that no one felt they owned the whole problem. Serendipity intervened. The American Cancer Society, the Centers for Disease Control and Prevention, and the National Cancer Institute of the National Institutes of Health asked the Academies to conduct a consensus study on a national strategy for cancer control.

A Committee on a National Strategy for Cancer Control in the USA was formed with Dr. Johns as Chair. I was a member of this committee. Most importantly, several systems-oriented thought leaders were recruited to the committee. The right people were in the room. This resulted in the 2019 National Academy report *Guiding Cancer Control: A Path to Transformation*.

The summary of the report

portrays cancer as a clustering of different diseases that afflict individuals in different ways. Its burdens are equally broad and diverse, from the physical, financial, and psychological tolls it imposes on individuals to the costs it inflicts upon the nation's clinical care and public health systems, and despite decades of concerted efforts, those costs have only continued to grow over time. The causes and effects of cancer are complex – in part preventable and treatable, but also in part unknown, and perhaps even unknowable.

The report

defines the key principles, attributes, methods, and tools needed to achieve the goal of implementing an effective national cancer control plan. It describes the current structure of cancer control from a local to global scale, identifies necessary goals for the system, and formulates the path towards integrated disease control systems and a cancer-free future. This framework is a crucial step in establishing an effective, efficient, and accountable system for controlling cancer and other diseases.

The body of the report articulates this framework in terms of a complex adaptive system.

Many committee members had been hesitant to embrace the construct of complex adaptive systems. The above list of characteristics seemed too abstract. This motivated me to draft a one-page table with two columns. The left column included the six characteristics listed above. The right column included the following:

- System responses often seem unpredictable and disproportionate to interventions. For example, enormous efforts are often needed to achieve small changes, while at times, small improvements in treatment might lead to significant changes in clinical care.
- Stakeholders (patients, families, clinicians, suppliers, payers, regulators, etc.) respond based on their perceptions, values, and priorities, which are seldom aligned (e.g., payers might try to constrain short-term costs even when long-term health and economic benefits are easily projected).
- Goals and behaviors of stakeholders often conflict. They may perceive these conflicts and adapt their strategies to counteract their impacts.

For example, enormous resources might be devoted to advertising to convince patients of their need for products or services with questionable benefits.

- As the rules of the system evolve and stakeholders understand the impacts of those rules, they might develop strategies to circumvent these rules, including lobbying to avoid rule changes or to change the rules to their benefit.
- Stakeholders adapt to the changing environment, learning what works and does not. These behaviors often surprise other stakeholders, who then also need to adapt. For example, industry agents might just pay penalties rather than change behaviors in response to rules in the system.
- The healthcare system is a federation of millions of entrepreneurs with no one in charge. No single entity can command change. A portfolio of motivations, incentives, and disincentives is needed but would be difficult to design and deploy, particularly if stakeholders game the process.

Discussion of this table during a committee meeting completely convinced the skeptics. This table was included in the final report.

Once the report was released by the Academies, a subset of the committee traveled to Congress to brief senior staff members of relevant House and Senate Committees. I was asked to present the notion of complex adaptive systems. I had anticipated the following question:

"Can you explain the implications of this report in one sentence?"

I responded, "Yes, think differently, play together."

Opioid Epidemic

In the 1980s, pain increasingly became recognized as a problem that required adequate treatment. Pharma's business model for pain pills included misleading advertising, an aggressive sales force, and incentives for doctors to prescribe opioids. Once addicted, people found heroin to be much cheaper than prescription drugs, and more powerful.

Unfortunately, the service supply chain for treating substance abuse is highly fragmented. Before the present epidemic, opioids were prescribed mainly for short-term uses such as pain relief after surgery or for people with advanced cancer or other terminal conditions. But in the USA, the idea that opioids might be safer and less addictive than was previously thought began to gain credibility.

Prescriptions for opioids increased gradually throughout the 1980s and early 1990s. In the mid-1990s, pharmaceutical companies introduced new opioid-based products. Of particular note is Purdue Pharma's OxyContin, a sustained-release formulation of oxycodone. Prescriptions surged and the use of opioids to treat chronic pain became widespread.

The structure of the healthcare system in the USA also contributed to the over-prescription of opioids. Because many doctors are in private practice, they can benefit financially by increasing the volume of patients that they see, as well as by ensuring patient satisfaction, which can incentivize the over-prescription of pain medication. Prescription opioids were also cheap in the short term. Patients' health-insurance plans often covered pain medication but not pain-management approaches such as physical therapy.

I conducted a series of interviews with front-line health professionals at MedStar Health in Baltimore. Interviewees included nurses, social workers, and recovery coaches. My interview notes include litanies of needs for better integration of care across health, education, and social services.

One nurse complained of the enormous percentage of time she spends on the phone trying to coordinate the services needed by patients. A social worker commented that substance abuse was typically just one of a patient's problems. Other problems included mental health challenges, joblessness, and homelessness. A recovery coach noted one patient who had been in the Emergency Department several hundred times over a two-year period.

There have been concerted efforts to limit opioid prescription in terms of both numbers of pills and refills. This will likely limit the growth of the number of new addicts. However, as noted earlier, it forces existing addicts to seek new and less safe sources of opioids and heroin. A much more integrated approach to population health is needed to assist these people.

Working with a research team at MITRE, we developed an agent-based model of the population of Washington, DC, at the level of each individual citizen, i.e., 700,000 agents. Based on thorough research of the medical literature, we developed a state-based model of each agent that included comorbidities and social determinants of health. A range of data sets were employed to tailor the agent models to the residents of each of the city's eight wards.

Our primary interest was in the extent to which social interventions, rather than medical interventions, could motivate addicts to enter recovery. In particular, we were intrigued by the impacts of peer recovery coaches reported in the medical literature. We hypothesized that an addict's likelihood of seeking recovery is related to the number of recovered addicts in their social network.

We used the model to predict the number of emergency room visits due to overdoses and the number of deaths due to overdoses for each ward. Our predictions were quite close to the actual data, including the wide variations between the poorer and more affluent wards. Unexpectedly and unfortunately, we were able to use the model to conduct a natural experiment described below.

Coronavirus Pandemic

The global pandemic of coronavirus disease (COVID-19) is caused by severe acute respiratory syndrome coronavirus (SARS-CoV-2). The novel virus was identified in Wuhan, China, in December 2019. It spread to other parts of mainland China and around the world. The World Health Organization (WHO) declared the outbreak a pandemic in March 2020. Variants of the virus have resulted in further waves in several countries. As of July 2021, more than 200 million cases have been reported, with more than 4 million confirmed deaths, making this one of the deadliest pandemics in history.

Our experiment involved predicting the impacts of social isolation, due to the coronavirus, on opioid abuse overdoses and deaths. We socially isolated the agents in our model. Thus, current addicts had no interactions with recovered addicts. The model predicted increases in overdoses and deaths. Our predictions were in the ballpark with what actually happened.

We are currently evaluating the impacts of a possible new vaccine that prevents opioid overdoses. This seems like a great idea but may backfire. If this vaccine greatly reduces the likelihood of overdoses, addicts may not be motivated to enter recovery. Thus, there will be fewer recovered addicts to convince current addicts to attempt recovery. The result may be more addicts.

EDUCATION

There seems to be widespread agreement that our societal system for delivering health and wellness needs substantial improvement in terms of outcomes achieved and, in particular, the costs of achieving these outcomes. These perceptions are much less common, but nevertheless highly relevant, for our system of education.

We have the best higher education system in the world, as evidenced by the huge numbers of international students that seek to matriculate in the USA, particularly for graduate studies. However, for a large proportion of US students, the education system does not work that well and is inordinately expensive.

A significant source of this underperformance is due to inadequate K–12 preparation. The 14,000 school districts in the USA are under local control with state support and minimal federal intervention. Consequently, a local school district can simply choose to not offer the courses necessary for K–12 graduates to become STEM-ready where STEM denotes science, technology, engineering, and math.

In Chapter 8, I discussed education emphasizing elementary, secondary, and post-secondary education, with particular emphasis on institutions of higher education. In this section, I consider education as a means of providing the workforce of the future.

Various pundits have argued that automation in general and artificial intelligence, in particular, will eliminate many jobs. I have seen estimates ranging from 25% to 50% of all jobs no longer needing human performers. Thus, perhaps 30–60 million jobs might disappear. No doubt, there will be jobs taken over by machines, but that has been the case since the Industrial Revolution.

My latest back-of-the-envelope projection is that at least 25 million new jobs will be created, perhaps many more than we can currently envision. A large portion of these jobs will be in what is characterized as the skilled technical workforce. These jobs will require strong technical skills to design, develop, operate, and maintain our increasingly complex systems.

These jobs will not require a BS in a STEM field but will require technical education, typically at a community college, followed by employer-based training specific to the particular systems that the employer develops, operates, or maintains. My very rough estimate is that the capacity of US community colleges will have to triple to create the needed workforce talent pipeline.

People with only high school education, and especially those without a high school diploma, will have great difficulties securing a middle-class income. There will be plenty of well-paying jobs, but, given our current educational system, millions of people will be unprepared for these jobs. Perhaps this will create opportunities for the academic ecosystem to create new educational pathways. The challenges outlined in Chapter 8 may provide the motivation to innovate.

ENERGY

There is emerging widespread agreement that climate change – sea level rise, increased temperatures, and violent storms – is due to carbon emissions from burning fossil fuels. We are faced with the dual challenges of mitigating carbon emissions while also mitigating the consequences of changes that have already happened. This endeavor can be facilitated by understanding the Earth as a system, as shown in Figure 10.1.

Loosely speaking, there are four interconnected systems: environment, population, industry, and government. In this notional model, population consumes resources from the environment and creates by-products. Industry also consumes resources and creates by-products, but it also

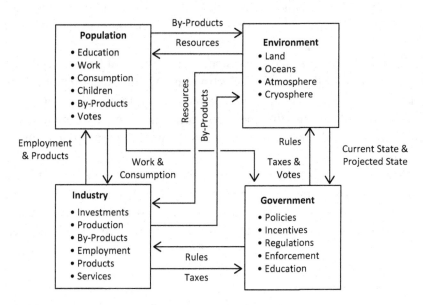

FIGURE 10.1
Earth as a System.

produces employment. The government collects taxes and produces rules. The use of the environment is influenced by those rules.

Global populations are "hooked on energy." Economic development is enabled by energy consumption. Automobiles, meat consumption, air conditioning, and constant connectivity are among the driving forces. How do we moderate these demands without undermining economic development?

Advanced technologies for reducing emissions and mitigating consequences are key, but how quickly and economically can these be adopted? A key question is whose incomes and livelihoods are disrupted and how can they be supported to sustain these disruptions? How can investors be compensated for massive investments now obsolete?

Battery Electric Vehicles

Substantial environmental and energy challenges are driving the pursuit of alternative powertrain technologies, which nominally includes engine, transmission, drive shaft, differential, and the final drive. Emerging alternative fuel vehicles are showing their potential to address these challenges. However, the diffusion of new technologies has many complications. We investigated the impacts of individual and organizational parameters on the adoption of battery electric vehicles (BEVs).

Chen Liu and I employed system dynamics modeling to create a representation of the automotive ecosystem. Mathematical relationships among different variables were derived. The impacts of government rebates, manufacturer willingness, and consumer purchasing preferences on economic and environmental issues were addressed using scenario analysis.

Three major stakeholders in the California automobile market were considered (government, manufacturer, and consumer). The types of powertrain systems considered included small-/mid-sized internal combustion engines (ICE), large-sized ICE, hybrid, BEV, and fuel cell electric vehicles. Near-term impacts of government rebates, both federal and state, were found to be important to launch the market.

However, the model suggested that long-term impacts will come primarily from product familiarity, consumer preferences, and technology competitiveness. This supports the importance of investments in R&D

and advertising. Such investments could be augmented by government support of manufacturers or related research organizations. Rather than depending on short-term rebates for consumers, fundamental improvements in technology and infrastructure, e.g., charging stations, provide more resilient ways to achieve long-term growth of this new technology.

Battery electric vehicles were found to be significantly more environmentally friendly if the electricity used to charge the vehicles was not produced by coal-fired electric plants. Green electricity generation will lead to larger and more stable environmental improvements in the long term. Furthermore, pure green electricity production affects CO_2 emissions beyond just vehicles. However, totally switching to green energy production in a short time is highly unlikely. Nevertheless, the model suggests the importance and value of paying more attention to changing production to green energy methods.

Autonomous Vehicles

The transportation industry is facing a revolution similar to when machines replaced animals one century ago. Humans may for the first time be fully out of the control loop of personal transportation. However, this revolution involves considerable disruption and uncertainty. Nevertheless, autonomous vehicles (AVs) will increasingly impact the automobile market.

Chen and I mapped various causal relationships during this significant transition to understand the impacts of different phenomena. A systems dynamic model was constructed including two different transportation methods (personal owned vehicle and car services) and three autonomy levels (non, semi, and full).

Consumer choices, product familiarity, and acceptance were modeled to represent purchasing behavior. The US auto insurance industry is likely to be substantially impacted by autonomous vehicles. Vehicle crash rate and loss ratio were considered to calculate the insurance industry's premium collections. Different scenarios were quantified and discussed with key stakeholders. Several important causal loops were identified that will help achieve the faster growth of the technology.

With gradually improving vehicle driving assistance technologies, AVs are expected to debut in this decade. As a revolutionary way of personal transportation, it is very promising from various perspectives, including enriching personal mobility, reducing energy consumption, and dramatically decreasing vehicle accidents. Yet, not everyone is optimistic.

A primary motivation for this effort was to understand the impacts of AVs on the insurance industry. Every state in the USA has regulations that limit auto insurance premiums to the costs of insurance claims. Thus, insurance companies do not make profits on premiums. They make money by investing the premium monies until these funds are needed to pay claims.

The model predicts that insurance industry premiums collected will continue growing until the penetration rate of AVs becomes significant. At that point, the frequency of accidents, and hence, claims, will decrease. Once the AV technology takes off, the industry premiums collected will be dramatically reduced.

Another consideration is the likelihood that people will use car services that own AVs rather than own the vehicles themselves. As these vehicles will be highly utilized, the total number of vehicles on the road will be reduced. Thus, the economic scale of the insurance industry will be further reduced, which will lead to decreased premiums collected. Reduced accidents and fewer cars on the road combine to result in substantial reductions in insurance premiums collected.

In many meetings with insurance industry executives, they characterized AVs as a major threat to their industry. Steadily decreasing accidents portend great social benefits, but stakeholders such as insurance companies, collision repair shops, and personal injury law firms will experience revenue losses. Innovations often result in the investors in the status quo suffering, and the complex adaptive system responds accordingly.

Climate Change

Humanity has always exploited natural resources for food, shelter, energy, etc. This exploitation emerged on an industrial scale in the 19th century as the extraction and processing of raw materials blossomed during the Industrial Revolution. During the 20th century, energy consumption rapidly increased.

Today, the vast majority of the world's energy consumption is sustained by the extraction of fossil fuels, including oil, coal, and gas. Intensive agriculture also exploits the natural environment via degradation of forests and water pollution. As the world population rises, the depletion of natural resources will become increasingly unsustainable.

Almost 90% of all human-produced CO_2 emissions come from the burning of fossil fuels like oil, coal, and natural gas. Deforestation also increases CO_2 in the atmosphere by destroying trees that consume CO_2. The CO_2 in the atmosphere increases greenhouse warming, which results when the atmosphere traps solar radiation. Consequently, the Earth's temperature increases. This leads to ice melting and sea level rise.

Beyond threatening coastal buildings, rising sea levels lead to salinization of groundwater and estuaries. This decreases the availability of freshwater. Ocean acidification also affects sea life. Consequently, the food supply and human health are degraded.

A multi-faceted approach to CO_2 reduction involves reducing, reusing, and recycling. Using less heat and air conditioning, using less hot water, replacing incandescent light bulbs, and buying energy-efficient products are elements of this approach. Using the off switch on lights and appliances is also of value.

Transportation is a large producer of CO_2. Compared to an average single-occupant car, the fuel efficiency of a fully occupied bus is six times greater and a fully occupied train car is 15 times greater. In general, we need to drive less and ride smarter. Increased migration to cities should help this, as the feasibility of mass transit increases with population density.

Urban living is, in general, more energy efficient than suburban or rural living. For example, apartment living involves more shared walls and fewer exposed walls, reducing energy consumption for heating and cooling. Green spaces in cities are also important both for people's well-being and the CO_2 that trees consume.

We cannot deal with global warming by simply restoring everything that is damaged, and then restoring it again after the next flood, for example. We either have to stem the use of fossil fuels or prepare for disruptive and eventually different living conditions. Fortunately, these dire possibilities are now receiving substantial attention.

We have been exploring model-based approaches to assess the likely impacts and costs of alternative approaches to addressing climate change, in terms of mitigating both the causes and consequences. Modeling this complex adaptive system is an enormous challenge. There are many researchers pursuing a wide range of models. Connecting these pieces of the puzzle is a fundamental challenge in itself, as I discussed in Chapter 9.

TRANSFORMATION

At some point, process improvement is no longer sufficient and transformation is needed, as I discussed in Chapter 7. This is a very significant challenge at an enterprise level, but an enormous challenge for society. Masses of people have arranged their lives based on assumed continuity of employment, incomes, etc. All these masses vote and are opposed to disruption. Politicians understand this and aspire to reelection.

Yet, fundamental change does occasionally happen. It is more common in private enterprises where market forces play predominant roles. It is less common in public enterprises, and public–private ecosystems, but it does happen when a variety of forces align to motivate and invest in change. We are not good at this, but we occasionally pull it off.

Transformative public sector innovations in the health domain have included Social Security, Medicare and Medicaid, and the Affordable Care Act. In education, transformative innovations have included the Morrill Land Grant Acts, the GI Bill following World War II, and the formation of the National Science Foundation. In energy and climate, innovations have included the formation of the National Oceanic and Atmospheric Administration and the Environmental Protection Agency, as well as the Corporate Average Fuel Economy (CAFE) standards.

Much can be learned from studying these innovations. What circumstances hindered or enabled the Congressional action? Certainly, coalitions of stakeholders played key roles. Nevertheless, several of these initiatives faced headwinds for decades. Persistence is obviously another important factor.

CONCLUSIONS

This chapter has outlined our endeavors to address complex societal systems. Health, education, and energy are not problems of single enterprises or even single domains. They involve people, families, and social networks that cut across domains. Many of the concepts and methods outlined in earlier chapters were applied to the problems discussed in this chapter. However, given the wicked nature of most of these problems, our conclusions cannot be as definitive. Further, these complex adaptive systems are more amenable to influence than control.

EPILOGUE

My intense involvement in Washington, DC, has taught me that you cannot expect to "fix" things. You can only aspire to enable and influence the needed discussions and debates. This requires a network of connections and a reputation as a trusted source of counsel and advice. It requires that you do your homework and stay on top of the latest findings and their implications.

Success in Washington, DC, is a team sport. You cannot know everything, but you can come close to knowing everybody associated with a particular issue or challenge. For me, a particularly intriguing aspect of this has been my natural tendency to approach everything as a research project. Being involved in endless meetings can be very tedious – especially if they are Teams or Zoom meetings – unless you approach each meeting as a data point on what was discussed, why did it matter, and whose position prevailed, if any.

Societal systems can be overwhelmingly complex if you approach them as you would physics or chemistry. The elements of a societal system may have some predictable behaviors, but they can surprise you, particularly if they perceive that you see them as predictable. Then, if only to keep you on your toes, they will say or do something you had not expected. That's how people win games, whether it is basketball, football, or politics.

FURTHER READING

Pate-Cornell, E., Rouse, W.B., & Vest, C.M. (Eds.).(2016). *Perspectives on Complex Global Challenges: Education, Energy, Healthcare, Security, and Resilience*. New York: Wiley.

Rouse, W.B. (2021). *Failure Management: Malfunctions of Technologies, Organizations, and Society*. Oxford, UK: Oxford University Press.

Rouse, W.B. (2022). *Transforming Public-Private Ecosystems: Understanding and Enabling Innovation in Complex Systems*, Oxford, UK: Oxford University Press.

Rouse, W.B., Boff, K.R., & Sanderson, P. (Eds.).(2012). *Complex Socio-Technical Systems: Understanding and Influencing Causality of Change*. Amsterdam: IOS Press.

11

Looking Back

The 50-year professional journey that I have chronicled in this book has provided me with a wealth of lessons learned. I have related many of these lessons in the preceding chapters. My objective in this chapter is to provide an integrated perspective of these varied lessons, including a few potential overarching lessons.

There are several types of lessons. You might learn something that was previously unknown to you. You could learn how this thing works in terms of inputs and outputs or equivalent. You might learn about how to affect this thing. You could seek to learn how behavioral and social phenomena affect it. The result could be the knowledge and skills that enable you to make a difference.

There are also lessons about where you can facilitate change and where you cannot. In some situations, you can know where a nudge will make a difference. In other situations, you can perceive where hardened perspectives will fight you. The key, I think, is to know where investments of energies and resources will pay off, and where such investments will not pay off.

I think the desires to have an impact increase with age. The notion of making a difference, if you are fortunate, can become more important than making a living. From this perspective, once you sense that your efforts are unlikely to make a difference, you can move on to other opportunities. Of course, you need to keep in mind that helping people to understand real problems, even if you cannot contribute to solving them, is an important contribution.

DOI: 10.4324/9781003365549-11

DESIGN, MANAGEMENT, AND POLICY

I have invested an enormous amount of energy trying to improve the returns on investments in human systems. The construct of human-centered design was my primary contribution to this endeavor, along with repeated demonstrations of the merits of this construct. These demonstrations provided evidence that the approach can make a difference.

The central premise in human-centered design is that everyone counts, not just the end users. The goal is to delight the primary stakeholders and gain the support of secondary stakeholders. This is a form of design inclusivity. Every idea counts and deserves a listen. Of course, only good ideas will survive. In fact, one of the strengths of the models discussed throughout this book is how they can help to get rid of bad ideas quickly.

What do you need to know about stakeholders? There are obvious things like their backgrounds and positions. More important are their values, concerns, and perceptions. What do validity, acceptability, and viability mean to them in the context of the problem at hand? It can be important to try to infer their mental models, needs, and beliefs.

A central concern is how to represent the phenomena underlying the problem of interest. I have found that multi-level models are often needed to capture the scope of these phenomena. Levels usually differ in terms of levels of abstraction (e.g., people, processes, organizations, and ecosystem) and in some cases levels of aggregation (i.e., systems, subsystems, assemblies, and components).

Models of phenomena at each level often need to be connected to models of phenomena at other levels. This can lead to the need to compose possibly incompatible representational paradigms. You may need to develop mechanisms to enable valid linkages. You will need to carefully articulate and manage the assumptions underlying these mechanisms.

Interactive visualizations of the multi-level models are central to stakeholder engagement. Such engagement is essential to making decisions and gaining commitments to their execution. These visualizations should support the model-based exploration of "What if?" questions. These interactive visualizations are often called policy flight simulators, which can be hosted in a version of an *Immersion Lab.*

The overall goal is to help stakeholders explore and understand complexity, often manifested as complex adaptive systems. The complexity of interest includes the technical system, the organizational system, and the social system in which the technical and the organizational systems are embedded. More broadly, the societal ecosystem also often informs the functioning of the other levels, at the very least in terms of values and norms.

There are a few overarching success factors. The first is stakeholder involvement. Next is a focus on the alignment of incentives across stakeholders. This may require broadening the agenda to involve other tradeoffs. Finally, it is important to identify and achieve early small wins. Tangible, albeit perhaps modest, indicators of progress are important so that stakeholders see that things are happening.

I have worked with well over 100 companies, agencies, and institutions. I have found that these lessons learned apply everywhere. They may be articulated differently in diverse contexts. However, the principles of human-centered design work everywhere. Now, consider what changes when addressing not a single enterprise or agency, but a whole ecosystem.

PUBLIC–PRIVATE ECOSYSTEMS

In contrast to single enterprises, whether they be private or public, the range of public–private ecosystems is immense. My native town of Portsmouth, RI, had 6,000 residents when I grew up and perhaps a couple of hundreds of town employees, at most, across school teachers, police, fire, and town hall. New York City has 325,000 employees – one-third of the number of people in the whole state of Rhode Island.

Consequently, in this section, I am not going to address public–private ecosystems in general. Instead, I will focus on those ecosystems that I have experienced. From this basis, I will speculate on generalizations across ecosystems. These generalizations might best be viewed as hypotheses rather than conclusions.

NATIONAL SECURITY

As I related earlier, I was commissioned in the Air Force 50 years ago, served a brief stint of active duty, and served two terms on the Air Force

Scientific Advisory Board. I have had the good fortune of receiving research contracts from the Air Force, Army, and Navy, as well as Defense Advanced Research Projects Agency (DARPA) and OSD (Office of the Secretary of Defense), for most of my career. Defense agencies and their laboratories are great sources of R&D funds.

These sponsors are willing to make bets on high-risk, high payoff ideas. DARPA epitomizes this risk-taking attitude. DARPA Challenges provide substantial monetary prizes for demonstrating, for example, that a driverless car can successfully negotiate a course through rugged terrain. DARPA Program Managers have tremendous latitude in making such investments.

So, there is plenty of money and risk taking, but I have found it very difficult to get results adopted. For example, we developed training systems for the Army for communications systems maintenance and the Navy for helicopter maintenance. We evaluated these systems and showed substantial improvement in the performance of Army and Navy trainees. The instructors asked if their organizations could buy these training systems. We offered them at no cost, but they could not accept them because they were not "approved training devices."

There is almost overwhelming organizational inertia. This is perhaps not surprising in the world's largest organization of 2 million employees. They face never-ending performance, schedule, and cost challenges with the systems they acquire. Political pressures are intense as defense budgets and contracts fund an enormous number of jobs, which Members of Congress seek to gain and retain in their districts and states.

The technological dominance of the defense ecosystem is waning, with private, non-defense, investments in R&D growing steadily. Many technological innovations now emerge in the commercial sector. Rates of technological change are much faster there, e.g., new iPhones every year. Defense can take two decades to acquire a new aircraft and keep it in service for the subsequent five decades. There is a significant mismatch of time scales.

Many years ago, I discovered a strategy for addressing this ecosystem. I pursue significant resources from defense research agencies – they are willing to invest much more than non-defense sponsors. We conduct the research and publish the results but do not expect the defense ecosystem to adopt our results. Instead, we approach non-defense stakeholders with our proven technologies and convince them to invest to take advantage of these capabilities. Interestingly, once we have innovated in a non-defense domain, the folks in defense have occasionally acquired our commercial solutions.

HEALTHCARE DELIVERY

Health and wellness provide an excellent example of transferring the results of defense investments to another ecosystem. My forays into healthcare delivery started at Tufts New England Medical Center in 1973 as I related earlier. This negative experience caused me to avoid the domain until the late 1990s when I engaged with the American Cancer Society to address strategic investment issues.

At that point, I learned about the difference between the science of medicine and the science of healthcare delivery. Researching and developing new medical treatments and drugs is different from figuring out how to affordably deliver these benefits to large populations of people. The difference was very clear in my work with the American Cancer Society. If all monies are invested in medical research, fewer patients benefit than if some of the monies addressed healthcare delivery.

Soon, I was heavily involved in the latter with the National Academy of Engineering and the Institute of Medicine (IOM), now the National Academy of Medicine. IOM recognized that the delivery system needs to be engineered. This collaboration continues today, as discussed in earlier chapters.

An early lesson was the extent to which local innovative practices do not inherently scale to widespread adoption. Two factors underlie this difficulty. Scaling success is inhibited by the lack of portable leadership, i.e., the originator of the innovation, who was often committed to success beyond reason, is not provided with the documentation of the practice.

Second, the substantial fragmentation of the US health delivery system seriously undermines the quality of care. Providers are trying to make money, payers are trying to save money, and suppliers are seeking market shares. Further, the rules of the game differ across states. Few of the players are seeking to provide high-quality integrated population health. Consequently, the adoption of proven innovations is not a priority.

The coronavirus pandemic has prompted changes. Telemedicine has prospered now that payers will reimburse for services provided in this manner. Constraints in practicing across state lines have weakened, particularly for telemedicine for veterans. These nonsensical constraints may reemerge as states seem determined to maintain local control, notwithstanding the detriments to their citizens. The political culture in some states avoiding vaccination and masks attests to this.

Overall, technological disruption is underway via sensors, data analytics, and artificial intelligence. Slowly but surely, the health and wellness ecosystem will be transformed to become more consumer driven. Patients and their families will not put up with poor quality, poor service, and expensive health services. The holds of the medical guilds on the health ecosystem will be broken once information on practices and outcomes are widely available – and a wide range of entrepreneurs are already doing this.

HIGHER EDUCATION

Guilds are not unique to healthcare. Education, particularly higher education, has deep traditions of guilds (or disciplines) that dominate curricula, hiring, promotion, and tenure. The traditional organizational model, i.e., colleges, schools, and departments, that originated in Bologna, Italy, in 1088, is still very strong. This was 300 years before the Vatican returned from Avignon to Rome. Why change something that seems to be working?

However, the costs of this organizational model have gotten out of hand. Provosts, vice provosts, assistant vice provosts, deans, associate deans, deputy associate deans, and senior executive assistants for everyone get expensive. The result has been tuition increases that have outstripped inflation due to the strong growth of non-instructional costs. These escalating costs are subsidized by enormous expansions of student debt. One well-known university system has the distinction of having one non-faculty administrator per student. Each student can, in effect, have their own personal administrator.

Markets cannot sustain such inefficiencies. Demands for US degrees, particularly graduate degrees, are diminishing, and foreign student cash cows are dwindling. This is due to the parity of other countries' institutions and US immigration challenges. More threatening is the ongoing technological disruption due, in particular, to high-quality, low-cost online delivery. Georgia Tech is offering a high-quality, very highly-ranked MS in computer science for $7,000 for the whole degree, compared to $30,000 for an in-person degree at Tech, or $60–80,000 at many private institutions. The eventual outcome is very clear. The pandemic has accelerated these consequences.

The current business model of higher education is unsustainable. Well, it may be sustainable for the top 50–100 of our 2,500 universities – those with substantial endowments and federal research funding. However, this is not the emerging reality for most of the higher education. Increased value at lower costs will dominate. It is highly speculative, but greatly enhanced K-12 education should be a priority. However, local taxpayers are unlikely to agree. The future of the country's workforce is a very low priority for payers of property taxes.

ENERGY AND CLIMATE

Energy is fascinating. We are all totally dependent on it. We use it for everything, ranging from our own metabolism, to photosynthesis, to our electrical outlets, and to the gas tanks or batteries in our vehicles. We have come to expect energy to be available when we need it. As side effects, however, we are heating the planet, melting the icecaps, warming the oceans, and changing global weather. The current situation is not sustainable.

A major contributor to global warming is carbon released by the burning of fossil fuels. Transportation is a substantial component of this. This has prompted a strong commitment to replacing internal combustion engines with electric motors. All of the major auto manufacturers have committed to this transition. I addressed the adoption by consumers of battery electric vehicles in Chapter 10. Driverless cars will also be electric, but they are still over the horizon.

This will reduce carbon emissions if the electricity used to charge these vehicles is not produced by coal-fired power plants. Electric utilities are usually regulated monopolies and not known for the agility of decision making or action. Nevertheless, in a current project in California, a public–private partnership is pursuing zero carbon by 2050. Fortunately, maturing renewable energy technologies are steadily becoming much less expensive, i.e., solar and wind. Hydropower is also renewable. Fourth-generation nuclear may be a possibility, but consumers are wary.

These trends are promising, but the delivery infrastructure is fragmented and fragile, as recently demonstrated in Texas. Further, the energy ecosystem is laced with strong vested industry and political interests. Major investments and 7 million jobs are at stake. Finally, there are strong and steadily increasing energy consumption habits of everyone globally.

The needs for change are increasingly widely recognized, but the path forward is complicated. The overall transition, which is not limited to vehicles and power generation, has to make sense for all the major stakeholders. This is complicated by the increasing prevalence of misinformation. The trust of expert information sources is critical, but, as demonstrated by the rejection of coronavirus vaccines by many, trust is currently in short supply.

I have written elsewhere that there will be no vaccine for rising sea levels. Nature will have its way, as it has with the pandemic. We need to anticipate and get ahead of looming crises. For the USA, this is not a strong suit. We tend to let bad things happen and then try to fix them. To an extent, this is why our response to climate change has been so slow. We deny problems until they are too overwhelming to avoid them any longer. The technologies to better anticipate and mitigate crises are increasingly available and affordable. We need the will to invest in these capabilities.

Above all, we need the will to honestly address the evidence at hand and grapple with alternative ways forward. The pronouncements of uneducated and ill-tempered pundits need to be labeled as such and broadly dismissed. This will require persistent public education. Politicians who dismiss this education should be ridiculed and turned out of office.

CONTRASTING ECOSYSTEMS

It is interesting to consider how these ecosystems are similar and different. To what extent are people generally familiar with each ecosystem? Certainly, people are very familiar with health and education, having personally experienced these domains. We are all significant consumers of energy, but many are likely less familiar with the energy industry. Without a doubt, people are much less knowledgeable of national security, other than simply having a sense of its general importance.

Market-driven competitive forces affect health and education. Energy, often a regulated monopoly, is slower to respond to competition. New entrants, either organizationally or technologically, can bring innovations to market to disrupt or perhaps displace incumbents. These three domains have competitors, but national security has adversaries. National security is not just seeking market share. Dominance is the goal.

What happens in each ecosystem? To what extent are these operations repetitive? Health, education, and energy involve doing the same things thousands and perhaps millions of times. National security tends to address potentially unique missions, which may be practiced but also may never occur. Consequently, it is inherently easier to learn in the health, education, and energy domains, and much more difficult for national security.

These ecosystems differ substantially in terms of the availability of data. Health and education publish findings of research studies in openly accessible literature. This is somewhat less common in energy but still significant. Data availability suffers in national security, due, in part, to information being classified, but also because, as noted above, national security does not involve doing the same things large numbers of times.

IMPLICATIONS

The many initiatives discussed in the earlier chapters involved similar concepts, principles, models, methods, and tools. Thus, these constructs are broadly applicable. However, this by no means suggests that everything can be engineered in the same ways.

Context really matters! The values, concerns, and perceptions of stakeholders in security, health, education, and energy differ dramatically. Human-centered design is premised on these enormous differences.

I suggest that the workbench is similar for all problems. The tools are similar, but the blueprints differ, often dramatically. A vanity table for a teenage daughter, stools for a young boy's pre-school teachers, and a chairside chest for grandparents involve very different plans, but the thinking and skills are common.

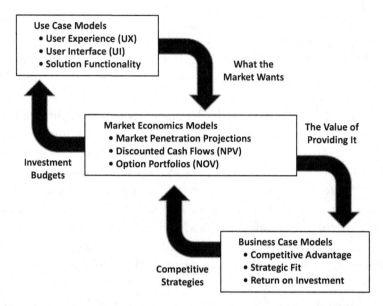

FIGURE 11.1
Model-Based Approach to Investments.

We design solutions for each other. This requires that we understand each other. Our preferences differ and we appreciate different attributes. However, we share a common aspiration to develop solutions that meet each other's needs. That is the essence of human-centered design. Everyone will be better off if we embrace this philosophy.

Figure 11.1 summarizes a model-based approach to investment analysis that I have found useful in the many domains I have discussed in this book. This approach involves iterative creation and exercising of interacting use case models, market economics models, and business case models. From a human-centered perspective, we always begin with the use case models.

LOOKING BACK

In hindsight, this 50+ year journey seems to make sense. One thing led to another in a seemingly orderly fashion. However, I could not have possibly envisioned this journey. Looking back, I am rather amazed. How did all that really happen? What caused these sequences of events?

It was all due to people and connections. Various mentors had confidence in me and facilitated opportunities. I took advantage of these opportunities and created valued outcomes, including lawns mowed, houses painted, software written, equations solved, products planned, and policies informed.

This required some level of intellectual ability and a willingness to work hard, but it also depended on encountering the circumstances where success was possible and taking advantage of these circumstances. Intellectual ability and a strong work ethic are necessary, but not sufficient. Somehow, you need the right circumstances.

My sense is that intellectual ability and a strong work ethic are more pervasive than we realize. What is often missing is the right circumstances. We need to better understand, and be better at, creating fortuitous circumstances for everybody. We need more mentors, looking out for young men or women where a bit of help will transform their lives.

Such transformations should be indelible functions of our culture. Fostering healthy, educated, and productive people can and should be a top priority. Assuring that everybody can succeed is a crucial step towards everybody actually succeeding. This is the essential mission of complex societal systems.

Index

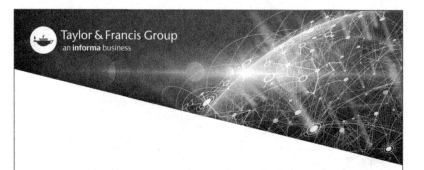

Printed in the United States
by Baker & Taylor Publisher Services